Red Auerbach: The Inspiring Life and Leadership Lessons of One of Basketball's Greatest Coaches

An Unauthorized Biography & Leadership Case Study

By: Clayton Geoffreys

Disclaimer: The following book is for entertainment and informational purposes only. The information presented is without contract or any type of guarantee assurance. While every caution has been taken to provide accurate and current information, it is solely the reader's responsibility to check all information contained in this article before relying upon it. Neither the author nor publisher can be held accountable for any errors or omissions. Under no circumstances will any legal responsibility or blame be held against the author or publisher for any reparation, damages, or monetary loss due to the information presented, either directly or indirectly. This book is not intended as legal or medical advice. If any such specialized advice is needed, seek a qualified individual for help.

Trademarks are used without permission. Use of the trademark is not authorized by, associated with, or sponsored by the trademark owners. All trademarks and brands used within this book are used with no intent to infringe on the trademark owners and only used for clarifying purposes.

This book is not sponsored by or affiliated with the National Basketball Association, its teams, the players, coaches, or anyone involved with them.

Visit my website at www.claytongeoffreys.com

Cover photo by Jack O'Connell is licensed under CC BY 2.0 / modified from original

Table of Contents

Foreword

Often considered one of the greatest team officials in professional sports history, Red Auerbach had an illustrious career as a basketball coach and executive. He is often credited for ushering in the foundational pieces of basketball today, with his abundant use of the fast break to create powerful offenses. Auerbach's work is clearly reflected in the mark he left on the Boston Celtics franchise, which included nine championships as a coach and seven more as an executive. Thank you for purchasing *Red Auerbach: The Inspiring Life and Leadership Lessons of One of Basketball's Greatest Coaches*. In this unauthorized biography and leadership case study, we will learn some of the background behind Red Auerbach's incredible life story, and more importantly his impact on the game of basketball. In the last section of the book, we'll learn what makes Red Auerbach such an effective leader and coach, including a review of key takeaways that you can remember when looking to apply lessons from Red Auerbach to your own life. Hope you enjoy and if you do, please do not forget to leave a review!

Also, check out my website at claytongeoffreys.com to join my exclusive list where I let you know about my latest books. To thank you for your purchase, you can go to my site to download a free copy of *33 Life Lessons: Success Principles, Career Advice & Habits of Successful People*. In the book, you'll learn from some of the greatest thought leaders of different industries on what it takes to become successful and how to live a great life.

Cheers,

Clayton Geoffreys

Visit me at www.claytongeoffreys.com

Introduction

Coaching has always been an art form in the world of basketball, and like most art, it evolves but traces its roots from the earlier pioneers of the craft. Of course, coaching always grew from some of the most successful systems, styles, and philosophies in the history of the sport. And as evident as it seems, dynasties are the result of some of the best coaching styles. History would show that there is no other dynasty more dominant and successful than the 1960's Boston Celtics.

While some would argue that the NBA was not as competitive or big as it was when the league was at its early stages, there can be no disputing that the Celtics of the 60's were utterly dominant. From 1957 to 1969, Boston was home to the NBA championship trophy eleven times, and no other team was as consistent as they were.

Since the league only had a few teams back then, several players of superstar talent were on the same team. The Los Angeles Lakers, San Francisco Warriors, Philadelphia 76ers, New York Knickerbockers, and St. Louis Hawks all had several stars on their roster. However, not one of those teams could even dethrone the Celtics, and it was not because Boston had the most talented players. The Celtics' team was a combination of skilled, talented, and unselfish players that knew their roles. Best of all, they were coached by a man that brought it all together for them.

Winning nine titles in a span of ten seasons, Red Auerbach was the architect of the Boston Celtics' dynasty during the 1960's. Their players may have been the soldiers out on the court and were just as talented as any other group of ballers in the NBA, but Red spelled the difference for the Celtics.

At a time when the NBA was still in its early stages concerning coaching, Red Auerbach revolutionized the art and helped make it to what it is today. He was the pioneer of several of today's simplest on-court principles such as the fast break and sixth man. He was also one of the first players to instill the importance of teamwork and selflessness.

During the 60's, when the NBA saw superstars that could put up 30 to 40 points a night while grabbing 20 rebounds per game, Red preached how crucial it was to never focus on statistics. He taught that every player had a role in the game and that nobody should ever put the team on their back on their own. Thus, he also became the pioneer of role players, who are guys on the team that have one specific task to do.[i]

Red Auerbach was also one of the first people to make the game more intense because of his fiery nature and attitude. He was never afraid to get the opposing team and players out of the game with his trash-talking and unabated temper. He always let people know what was on his mind and what he needed to say to help his team win games.

While Red Auerbach may have been a revolutionary character on the court, it was his off-court decisions that ultimately paved the way for the improvement of the game as a whole. At a time when the United States still had a barrier between people of different color and when the league and its fans favored white players, Red helped bridge the gap between races. In 1950, he drafted Chuck Cooper, the NBA's first African-American player. He would then continue to add more black players as the rest of the league followed suit. His philosophy for doing so was that he never cared about color. All he cared about was that he had talented and motivated players on his team.[ii]

In 1966, he made another decision that would change the face of NBA basketball. After stepping down from coaching to become the Celtics' general manager, he named Bill Russell as the team's head coach. His decision would make Russell the first African-American head coach in the NBA and the first black coach in professional sports since 1925. This paved the way for African-Americans to find themselves coaching not only in the NBA but for other major sports as well.

It was everything that Red Auerbach brought to the Boston Celtics on and off the court that eventually led them to become the league's most dominant dynasty in history. After winning nine titles during his time as a head coach, Red was the NBA's leader concerning championship rings for a head coach until Phil Jackson broke the record in 2010. However, no other head coach in the history of the league could claim to have won as many championships in so few years. Red Auerbach truly made the Celtics special in that era.

As Red Auerbach spent a lifetime winning titles both as a head coach and as the general manager of the Celtics, several coaches would follow in his footsteps to establish the same principles that he laid down when he was the head strategist in Boston. The fast break became the norm. Emphasis on superstars and isolation plays gave way to teamwork and ball movement. Coaches gave more importance to their bench and role players as teams became deeper and minutes became more spread out across the roster. And the NBA became more colorful because of how emotional Red was on the court and how he gave black players a chance to shine under the spotlight.

Truly one of the revolutionaries and pioneers not just of coaching but basketball itself, Red Auerbach has always had a special place in the history of the sport as the man that coaches would often look up to as an inspirational figure. Regarded as the best coach in the history of the NBA, Auerbach's influence can still be seen in how coaches today have instilled the same philosophies and concepts he pioneered back in the day. And when your influence spans decades and even centuries, that is when you know that you are a special figure in history.

Chapter 1: Background

Arnold Jacob Auerbach was born on September 20, 1917, in Brooklyn, New York at a time when basketball as a sport was still in its early stages. He was born to parents Marie and Hyman Auerbach. Hyman had Russian and Jewish backgrounds before he migrated to the United States. The patriarch of the Auerbach household helped his family get by as an owner of a deli and a dry cleaning business. Meanwhile, the American-born Marie worked at the deli.[iii]

The young Arnold Auerbach, who grew up in Williamsburg in Brooklyn, would later get his nickname "Red" because his hair was partly red. Red, who used to be called "Reds," played a lot of basketball in Brooklyn as a child since Williamsburg was one of the areas where the sport grew to be popular during the 20's and the 30's. However, his first taste of organized basketball was in Public School 122 in Brooklyn. In high school, later played on the varsity team of Eastern District High School.[iii] As a senior, he made the second team all-scholastic.[iv]

Red Auerbach was lucky to be in Brooklyn during that era of basketball. An old league called the American Basketball League (ABL) operated from 1925 to 1931. And at that time, Brooklyn had two of the professional teams that played in the ABL. They were the Brooklyn Arcadians and the Brooklyn Visitations. However, the two teams eventually disbanded because of the Great Depression. During that era, professional basketball in Brooklyn did not survive the hardship of the times. However, that did not deter Red Auerbach's love for the sport. He even organized basketball events for his local team, the Pelicans, despite the Depression.

The 5'9" guard that played for Eastern District High School loved the sport as a young player but only did so out of sheer circumstance. In Williamsburg, Brooklyn, people hardly played football or baseball at that time because they were too expensive amidst the Depression. It was difficult to maintain a team because of the need for huge practice fields. Because of those circumstances, young boys like Red were drawn to basketball. Hyman did not even approve of his son's choice of the sport but did not tell him to quit nonetheless.[iii]

In 1935, Red Auerbach attended Seth Low Junior College but would later realize that he wanted to pursue a career as a coach and teacher. He would only spend one year in that college before moving to George Washington University on a scholarship when a coach saw how well he played for Seth Low Junior College. He was a standout player there, though not everyone loved the way he played.[i]

Red Auerbach brought the same street ball style that made him a star in Brooklyn. However, his opponents and teammates did not always favor his style because of how organized basketball was in Washington. However, he lettered for three seasons in GW. But it was during his senior year in college when the foundation for his future philosophies was erected.

Other than leading his team in scoring as a senior, Red Auerbach would learn how to play a fast paced style of basketball under his coach William "Bill" Reinhart.[iii] As a senior, he saw the advantages of throwing long passes after a rebound to create a numbers advantage over at the other end. However, Auerbach would not have a very successful college career. His team went 38-19 in his three seasons at George Washington University.

After graduating from GW, Red Auerbach stayed with the university to pursue his Master's degree. During that time, he spent a portion of his life as a basketball director and coach of St. Albans, one of the prominent high school programs in Washington, D.C. At that time, he already saw that his future was as a coach instead of a player. That was the reason why he decided to go into coaching as early as his 20's.

Red Auerbach earned his Master's degree from GW in 1941 and married his wife Dorothy Lewis in the same year. He would then pursue a career as a high school teacher in Roosevelt High School in the D.C. area. He taught history and physical education during that time. He also spent time as a publisher of several basketball and physical education books. Red supplemented his income by working part-time as a referee. However, his career would be put on hold when he joined the Navy from 1943 to 1946.[iii]

Auerbach's love for physical education, sports, and basketball transcended into his service years in the Navy. Red was assigned to help the conditioning of his fellow Navy servicemen. And when he was assigned to Norfolk, where his old college coach was assigned, he coached the basketball team. He went on to beat the Washington Bears, a team of all African-Americans, twice, although that team had won a world tournament in Chicago earlier in 1943. After that, he was discharged from the navy when he experienced what it was like to coach professional basketball.

Chapter 2: NBA Career

Coaching

When Red Auerbach was coaching in the Navy, one of the people that saw how good he was as a coach was Mike Uline. Uline was a multi-millionaire that owned an arena in Washington. After Auerbach was discharged from service in 1946, Uline offered him a job as a coach for the Washington Capitols in the newly-formed Basketball Association of America (BAA), a precursor to the current NBA. However, Red Auerbach hesitated on the job because of how risky it was to focus on a newly-formed basketball league, especially given that he also had a $3,000 job waiting for him back in Roosevelt High School. Uline matched the offer by tendering Auerbach a $5,000 salary, and the rest was history.

Red Auerbach was free to assemble his team to his liking in the BAA's inaugural season in 1946 because Uline admitted that he had no idea how to run a team. However, Auerbach's vast knowledge of basketball and of the geography of where players of different skill levels come from proved to be invaluable. Other owners formed their teams by recruiting players from the local markets. Red, on the other hand, took players from different cities and states knowing that he could create a team with diverse skill sets.[i]

With a team full of different players that he scouted from all over the country, Red Auerbach had a successful first season as the Washington Capitols' head coach. After playing 60 games that season, the Capitols won 49 of them thanks to Red's leadership. They were also able to compile records that remained unbeaten in the BAA/NBA for a few seasons.

The Capitols finished the season with an 81.7% winning percentage, which stood as a BAA/NBA record until the Wilt Chamberlain Philadelphia 76ers broke it in 1967. In 1946, the Capitols also compiled a 17-game winning streak, which was unbeaten for more than two weeks. Starting the season 15-0, the Washington Capitols also had the BAA/NBA best start to the season for nearly seven decades until the 2015-16 Golden State Warriors broke the record.

Red Auerbach would lead the Washington Capitols to a first-place finish in the Eastern Division when the BAA only had 11 teams. However, the Capitols would end up losing after six games in a seven-game series to the Western Division leaders, the Chicago Stags. It was the Philadelphia Warriors who ended up winning the first-ever BAA championship by beating the Stags in five games.

The BAA would diminish during the 1947-48 season after four teams disbanded due to a combination of financial and logistical problems. But despite how the league got smaller, competition got tougher for Red Auerbach and the Washington Capitols. After being assigned to the Western Division that season, the Capitols only won 28 out of the 48 games they played and finished second in the division. They would lose to the Stags again in the playoffs.

Returning to the East during the 1948-49 season, the Washington Capitols were back to their comfort zone. Red Auerbach would lead the team to a 38-win season despite how the league grew larger when several National Basketball League (NBL) teams made the jump to the BAA. This time, Red would not be denied of an appearance in the BAA Finals but would end up losing to the Minneapolis Lakers and 6'10" center George Mikan, who was then basketball's most dominant player.

In 1949, the BAA and NBL merged to become the NBA after several of the latter's teams ended up jumping to the rival league. The 1949-50 season became the official inaugural season of the NBA. However, Red Auerbach, one of the best coaches in basketball, almost ended up not being part of the NBA's first season because of how he and Uline could not see eye-to-eye with a contract extension. Because of this, Red jumped to college basketball to become an assistant with Duke.

However, the owner of the Tri-Cities Blackhawks, who played in three cities Iowa, contacted Red Auerbach as he thought that his team needed a new head coach after starting their inaugural season in the Tri-Cities on a tough note. But Auerbach's stint with the Blackhawks, who would later be known as the Atlanta Hawks, was short-lived after he found out that one of his favorite players got traded without his approval. They would finish with a record of 28-29 in Auerbach's only losing season as a head coach before he eventually stepped down and quit the job.[iii]

After those brief stops in Washington, Duke University, and Iowa, Red Auerbach found a job as the new head coach of the Boston Celtics after president Walter A. Brown nearly gave up on the team due to losses and financial problems. In a sense, Auerbach was there to save the Celtics' fate. The Boston Celtics, in turn, saved Red as he found the home he had been longing for in the NBA.

The decision to hire Red Auerbach came after Brown consulted the Boston media. He was well aware that he had no idea of what to do in the world of sports and basketball and candidly asked the writers who he should consider for the new head coaching job. The group of sports writers did not hesitate to voice their opinion that the newly-available Red Auerbach was the best for the job. Walter A. Brown would then make the best decision in Boston Celtics history by hiring the future legendary coach.

Red Auerbach's first job was to make sure the Boston Celtics were going to be competitive entering the 1950-51 season. He had to improve the roster's talent by signing players in the 1950 draft. His first chance to do so was when Bob Cousy, New England's most talented and popular player, was available. However, Auerbach was not a fan of his flashy playing style and chose to pass on him in the first round.[v]

Red Auerbach had no assistants at that time. He was all alone on the coaching staff. He had to organize all the practices and also did all the scouting of opponents and college prospects. And when he began scouting Cousy, he decided that he did not want the Holy Cross All-American because of his flashy style of play. Bob Cousy was the progenitor of all flashy guards. He was the first to dribble the ball behind his back and was also the first to master the no-look pass. Auerbach did not like this style of play and decided not to use the Celtics' first-round pick on him. He did, in fact, receive a lot of criticisms for drafting 6'11" Chuck Share. He did so because he thought that the Celtics needed a center in a big man's league. Share would not even play for Boston.[v]

In the second round, Red Auerbach would make history. Regarded as a colorblind head coach that only focused on talent, work ethic, and motivation, Red Auerbach never cared about a player's color at a time when there were racial barriers between white and black Americans. He would then draft the NBA's first African-American player, Chuck Cooper, who paved the way for black players to come to the league. It was all thanks to Red Auerbach that African-Americans found a place in the NBA even when there was racial discrimination at that time in the United States of America.[iv]

The Celtics were coming into the 1950-51 season contented with the talent they had in the draft. However, they were far from done. Even though Red Auerbach initially passed on Bob Cousy, the flashy passer would eventually find his way to the Boston Celtics. The Tri-Cities would end up drafting him in the fourth round as he did not have the hype that other players such as George Mikan had as a college player. However, he was traded to the Chicago Stags after he refused to report to the Blackhawks. But the Stags would fold before the start of the season, and their players had to be distributed to the other teams. Fate would play its part when Walter A. Brown ended up drawing Cousy's name. Auerbach would say that they were "stuck" with Bob Cousy because of those incidents.[v] But it was "bad luck" that would eventually pay dividends for the team.

While Big Ed Macauley was Red Auerbach's top scorer that season, it was Bob Cousy who steered the Boston Celtics forward. Cousy disregarded how Red had previously called him a "local yokel" and would instead play hard for the Celtics. Dubbed as the "Houdini of the Hardwood, Bob Cousy was making passes unseen and never done before in the NBA. His no-look passes and behind-the-back dribbles got crowds excited. He also found open shots for his teammates at a high rate.

Red Auerbach led the Boston Celtics to a 39-30 season a year after the team won only 22 games. The Celtics were one of the best teams to watch on the floor and became known for sharing the ball under Red's philosophy of team play. However, they would eventually fall to the New York Knicks in two games in the Eastern Division Semifinals.

Despite that, Red Auerbach laid the groundwork for what was soon to become a dynasty in the NBA.

During the 1951-52 season, Red Auerbach's roster became more stable. Red bolstered the Celtics' scoring after adding future Hall of Fame player and All-Star Bill Sharman to the team. His team was ten men deep, and almost everyone on the team got a chance to display their skills. That season, Bob Cousy evolved into the league's premier superstar guard, finishing third in the NBA in scoring.

Under Red Auerbach that season, the Celtics would once again make the playoffs with a 39-27 record. During that season, the Boston Celtics became known for their electrifying offense as Red slowly introduced the importance of the fast break. The Celtics were the league leaders in points per game and pace because of how fast they tried to play every night. It also helped that Auerbach focused more on pushing and sharing the ball on every possession, though Cousy was the orchestrator of nearly all of their offensive sets. However, they would still end up losing to the New York Knickerbockers once again in the Division Semis.

Though the Celtics continued to improve every season as their core of Bob Cousy, Ed Macauley, and Bill Sharman never slowed the pace, Red Auerbach would still somehow face failure in the playoffs. In 1953, they would take down the Syracuse Nationals in the Division Semis but once again lost to the Knicks in the next round. And during the 1954 playoffs, they would lose to the Nationals in the Division Finals. It was the same story after the 1954-55 season when they lost to Syracuse in the Division Finals once again. Then, in 1956, after the Celtics lost to the Nationals in the Division Semis, Red Auerbach decided to make a change to his team.

On the day of the 1956 NBA Draft, Red Auerbach decided to break up his core by trading away his center Ed McCauley and Cliff Hagan to the St. Louis Hawks, the former Tri-Cities Blackhawks, to try to acquire college basketball's most dominant big man. However, even after the trade, the Rochester Royals were still picking ahead of Red Auerbach and the Boston Celtics. To try to persuade the Royals' owner to draft another player instead, Red offered the popular Ice Capades show to the Royals for free for one week. At a time when basketball was not as lucrative as it is today, it was a good deal for the Royals to accept a money-making show such as the Ice Capades. The Royals would honor their word and draft Sihugo Green instead.[iii]

After the trade, Bill Russell, a perennial winner in college basketball because of his dominant play, made his way to the Boston Celtics when he was drafted second overall. In the same year, Red would also draft Tom Heinsohn and KC Jones, who would become big contributors to the Celtics' upcoming dynasty. It was the dawn of a new age for Red Auerbach's Boston Celtics.

Though Russell was only available to the Celtics in the final 48 games of the season because he still had duties to the Olympic team sent to Melbourne, he became a vital part of Red Auerbach's system. Because Red always promoted the importance of team play and role specialization, everyone on the Celtics' roster had a specific job to do in their fast-breaking style.

Bill Russell initiated the fast break on the defensive end. He was the best defensive center in the league and arguably of all time. Russell used his defensive efforts to stop opponents from getting to the basket using his ability to seal off the lane and block shots. And because nobody in the NBA could rebound the ball as well as he did, the Celtics always secured possession of the missed shots as the other players would run off to the other end of the floor waiting for a pass from Bob Cousy and the other guards.

Because of the Celtics' all-around play and defensive intensity led by Bill Russell, Boston won 44 out of the 72 games they played that season. Red Auerbach's fast-breaking style made the Celtics the top offensive team in the league as six of his players averaged double digits in scoring. At that time, having four players scoring at least ten points was already rare because of how teams focused more on putting the ball in their superstars' hands. And because Cousy was the quarterback of that offensive attack, he was the first player under Auerbach to win the MVP award.

However, Auerbach had a different mindset. He never allowed his players to hog possession of the ball and instead focused more on ball movement and equal opportunities. Cousy, Sharman, Russell, and Heinsohn all had enough talent to put up 20 to 25 points a night but instead focused more on their role for the team rather than on scoring. He even empowered his bench players to step up. Back then, other teams hardly used their bench players, but Red allowed Frank Ramsey to contribute a lot to the team as their best scoring option off the bench. Ramsey would become one of the first players in the league to carry the mantle of the sixth man.

Red Auerbach would lead the Boston Celtics to a Division Finals win for the first time in franchise history when they swept their tormentors for several seasons the Syracuse Nationals. They would make the NBA Finals for the first time in franchise history after beating the Nationals in only three games. The Celtics were even better in the playoffs, and everyone seemed to have elevated their game.

The Boston Celtics would meet the St. Louis Hawks in the NBA Finals, where Red Auerbach showcased his famous fire for the game of basketball. During the series against the Hawks in St. Louis, Red would use a tape measure to see if the Celtics' basket was the same height. Insulted by Auerbach's insinuations that they were cheating, the Hawks' owner challenged the Boston Celtics' head coach. Red would famously clock his former boss on the mouth to show that he did fear anyone and that he would do anything to protect his team.[i] The Celtics would eventually win the NBA Finals for the first time in franchise history after beating the Hawks in seven games.

The following season, the Boston Celtics would remain one of the best teams in the entire league because of their offensive attack and defensive mastery of the paint thanks to Bill Russell, who was named MVP that season. They would once again make it to the NBA Finals after beating the Philadelphia Warriors in five games. However, they would fall to the St. Louis Hawks in six games in a rematch of the 1957 NBA Finals. But after that loss, it would take nearly a decade until the next time that Red Auerbach would not win a title at the end of the NBA season.

During the 1958-59 season, the Boston Celtics improved even more as a team. Nearly seven players averaged in double digits. Out of those seven players, two would score over 20 points while Tom Heinsohn barely missed that mark. It was a team built to run and share the ball as Red Auerbach led them to a 52-win season and to a 4-0 sweep of the Elgin Baylor-led Minneapolis Lakers in one of the foundations of what became a rivalry between the two teams. For the second time in three seasons, Red was a champion head coach.

The 1959-60 season saw the arrival of Wilt Chamberlain, who was immediately the most dominant player in the world and the epic rival of Bill Russell. But even though the competition between players increased, the Boston Celtics were still unbeatable as they went on to finish the season with a 59-16 season. They scored almost 125 points a night, a number that is difficult to achieve even in today's game, while six players averaged at least ten points. Russell, Cousy, Heinsohn, and Sharman all contributed about 20 points per game.

Red Auerbach would coach the Boston Celtics in a hard-fought Division Finals against the Philadelphia Warriors led by rookie MVP Wilt Chamberlain, who was putting up numbers nobody else in the league ever saw. But even though Wilt was a one-man team, he could not beat a Celtics squad that had seven players sharing the ball and playing off of one another. This was a classic example of how teamwork triumphs over individual play no matter how dominant it seems. Bill Russell and the Celtics would beat Wilt Chamberlain and the Warriors in six games. And in the Finals, Auerbach would meet the Hawks for the third time in four seasons and would beat them in seven games to win his third championship.

The Boston Celtics continued their dominance over the league thanks to how Red Auerbach preached team play. His roster was ten men deep, and only Russell was averaging heavy minutes. During the 1960-61 season, they would beat the Syracuse Nationals in the Division Finals in five games before beating the Hawks 4-1 in the NBA Finals to claim Red's third straight title. The year after that, the Celtics scratched the 60-win mark for the first time and would once again dominate the league. However, they faced fierce competition in the playoffs and needed seven games to beat the Warriors in the Division Finals and the Lakers in the NBA Finals. Nevertheless, Red Auerbach was a champion coach for a fourth consecutive season.

As the years went on and age caught up with guys such as Bob Cousy and Frank Ramsey, the Celtics continued to dominate the NBA because they were more than the sum of their players. Everyone on the team was interchangeable because of how effective their offensive attack and defensive intensity were. Even when Cousy retired in 1963 after winning the title for a fifth straight year, five become six the year after, and then six became seven. And finally, in 1966, he won his eighth straight and final title as the head coach of the Boston Celtics. In a span of ten seasons, Red Auerbach won nine championships for the Celtics.

After the 1965-66 season, Red Auerbach retired from his head coaching duties and assumed the role as the team's general manager. He had previously announced his decision during the season and would tell all other coaches that it was their last chance to take a shot at him.[i] But nobody even had a chance to beat him since he won his ninth title after that season.

Red Auerbach would name Bill Russell as his replacement during 1966 championship series versus the Los Angeles Lakers. Russell not only became a playing coach but was also the first African-American head coach in the NBA. But even after Red retired as a head coach, the Celtics continued to win two more titles in the next three seasons because the NBA's winningest head coach had already laid the foundations for success.

Team Executive

Red Auerbach announced his retirement from the Boston Celtics' head coaching duties during the 1965-66 season and said that it was going to be the last time other coaches could have a crack at him. He would assume the role of the Celtics' general manager but would make his first decision before his retirement as a head coach. One of his first moves as the general manager was during the 1966 Finals against the Los Angeles Lakers. He appointed Bill Russell as the Celtics' head coach starting in the 1966-67 season. Russell's appointment to such a duty made him the first

African-American head coach not only in the NBA but also in America's four major professional sporting leagues (NBA, NFL, NHL, MLB).

While Russell would fail to win the NBA title in 1967 when they lost to the Chamberlain-led Philadelphia 76ers, they would win two consecutive titles in 1968 and 1969. Bill Russell would retire after the 1968-69 season, and Red would replace him with his former player Tom Heinsohn. Under Heinsohn, however, Auerbach's Celtics saw periods of struggles.

While the Heinsohn-led Celtics missed the playoffs for two consecutive seasons, Red Auerbach quickly rebuilt the team because of the great pickups he had in the draft. One of his most classic moments as a general manager was when he drafted Dave Cowens. He scouted Cowens, the Florida State star, because he thought he had the makings of the next Bill Russell. He knew that Florida State did not get a lot of media coverage because of their suspension from the NCAA. But even though Cowens did not get a lot of attention, Red would storm out of one of Florida State's games looking like he did not like what he saw. He would dissuade other teams from scouting Cowens by saying, "I've seen enough," before leaving the game. Because other teams seemingly thought Dave Cowens was not worth their time, Red Auerbach would draft him in 1970.

Auerbach-drafted players such as Jo Jo White, Dave Cowens, Don Chaney, and Paul Westphal helped a Boston Celtics team built around John Havlicek get back to playoff contention. This team would win the NBA championship in 1974 and 1976 when the league was quickly becoming more competitive with the influx of new teams.

Near the end of the 70's era, the Boston Celtics would somehow fall into a slump as age caught up with John Havlicek and Red Auerbach had to let go of core players such as Paul Silas and Paul Westphal. This ultimately led to losing seasons, and Auerbach himself admitted that he should have kept Silas, who their best player and who Dave Cowens wanted to keep around.[vi] Things got worse when 13-time All-Star and face of the franchise in the post-Russell era, Havlicek, retired after the 1977-78 season. But similar to a few years ago when the Celtics struggled for a few seasons, Red Auerbach would easily bring Boston back on track.

During the offseason of 1978, owners that controlled the Celtics after Walter A. Brown passed away a decade and a half before had misunderstandings with Red Auerbach. Auerbach thought that John Y. Brown, the controlling owner, was too meddlesome. Sending three first-round picks to the New York Knicks for former All-Star but often-injured big man Bob McAdoo without Auerbach's knowledge was the last straw, and Red almost accepted an offer from the New York Knicks to become their new team executive.[vii]

However, the cab ride that Red Auerbach took on his way to the airport was the determining factor that made him stay in Boston. The cab driver got to him and told him how much Bostonians loved Red despite knowing how much trouble he had with the team owners. Red Auerbach ultimately decided to stay but still took the plane to New York to politely decline the offer.[vii] Red Auerbach would return to Boston and announce to the world that he was not going anywhere and that the Celtics would become great once more when they drafted Larry Bird.

Red Auerbach waved his magic wand once again when he took advantage of an NBA loophole at that time. Larry Bird was already eligible for the 1978 NBA Draft because his original college class of 1974 was already graduating. However, Bird still had one year left after transferring to Indiana State University. He was a favorite at the top overall spot, which the Indiana Pacers owned. However, the Pacers did not draft Bird because the latter had told them that he wanted to stay in college for his fifth year because his mother wanted him to graduate.

At that time, Indiana State did not get a lot of media attention. Because of this, Larry Bird was a virtual unknown to anyone other than Indiana natives. But Red Auerbach did his homework and saw that he had the makings of the next great Celtic superstar. Auerbach wanted hardworking superstars that could take any role. He knew that Bird was a gifted shooter, rebounder, and passer, and could be a good fit for just about any role on the team. And when teams who did not know how good of a player

Bird was passed on him, Auerbach took advantage and drafted him with the sixth overall pick of 1978.[viii]

Larry Bird would eventually lead ISU to a 33-0 record to reach the NCAA Finals game. The standout senior would face his future NBA rival Magic Johnson and Michigan State in the championship game, which Indiana State ultimately lost. Nevertheless, the way Bird took the nation by storm made Red Auerbach look like a genius. But nobody was surprised after he had spent a career drafting players with hidden Hall of Fame potential such as Bill Russell, John Havlicek, and Dave Cowens.

After the title game, Red wanted Bird to join a desperately losing Boston Celtics team in the season's final month. However, Bird declined to sign that season because he wanted to finish his degree and because he was having fun in college. He even put in a lot of extra work on his game after he mangled a finger in his shooting hand. All this ultimately led to a Boston Celtics resurgence during the 1979-80 season.

Larry Bird made Red Auerbach look like a genius once more when he finally joined the Celtics in 1979. He would lead Boston to a 32-win turnaround from the previous season as the Celtics won 61 games in his rookie year. However, Bird and the Celtics would lose to the Philadelphia 76ers in the Eastern Conference Finals. Nevertheless, Red was the author of the Celtics' quick return to title contention.

Red Auerbach had previously stated that the Boston Celtics were merely one or two moves away from title contention after signing Larry Bird in 1979.[ix] Those one or two moves would end up being one of the most lopsided moves in league history as he would orchestrate the trade that would complete the Boston Celtics' legendary 80's core trio.

In 1980, the Boston Celtics owned the top overall draft pick by their dismal 1978-79 season. But Auerbach had other plans in mind. He coveted the Golden State Warriors' seven-foot center, Robert Parish. Red used the first and 13th pick to bring in Parish and the third overall pick in what would ultimately become a lopsided move. The Warriors traded Joe Barry Carroll, who would have a respectable NBA season, while Red Auerbach drafted Kevin McHale with the third overall pick. Trading for Parish and drafting McHale completed what would soon become the Boston Celtics' Big Three.[ix]

It was a genius move by Auerbach. He thought that McHale was the best fit for the team among the 1980 draft hopefuls. However, he did not want to draft him with their top overall pick without getting anything in return. Instead, he went on to use that first overall pick as leverage to get Parish and place the Celtics in position to draft Kevin McHale because of that third pick from the Warriors. Nobody thought McHale would become the best player out of that class. However, Auerbach knew how great of a workhorse the Minnesota product was and realized that none of the other teams in the league thought he was the best player in that class. Once again, Red looked like a genius with the move that would soon be dubbed as "The Steal of the Century."

After that genius move by Red Auerbach, the Boston Celtics would win the 1981 NBA title under head coach Bill Fitch. The Celtics would remain one of the best teams in the NBA but would ultimately become the most dominant Eastern Conference franchise after Red traded for point guard Dennis Johnson in 1983 to complete the core that won the 1984 NBA championship.

Red Auerbach would relinquish his role as the team's general manager and became the Celtics' president in 1984 after the team won the championship. One of his biggest moves as team president was trading away popular guard Gerald Henderson, who was one of their key players in that 1984 championship win, in 1984 to the Seattle SuperSonics in exchange for what would become the second overall pick in 1986.

Since the Boston Celtics won the 1986 NBA title, Red Auerbach had seemingly covered the franchise's future as a contender by drafting Maryland standout big man Len Bias. As the core Big Three of Bird, Parish, and McHale were heading into their 30's, Red thought that Bias would become the player that would ensure that the Celtics would remain competitive in the 90's. Bias would, unfortunately, pass away shortly after he was drafted.

While the Boston Celtics remained competitive during the final years of the 80's, they would fail to win another title after that 1986 championship run. Age would catch up with the core trio of the team as Bird, McHale, and Parish moved past their prime. Larry Bird would retire at the end of the 1991-92 season, and McHale would follow the season after. Though the Celtics seemingly had a player they could count on in Reggie Lewis, he would, unfortunately, pass away due to heart problems in 1993.

Age caught up with Red Auerbach, and he admitted that he had lost interest in managing the Boston Celtics on a hands-on basis during the early 90's. Because he was getting older, Red would shift his focus to his hobbies and would leave the management to younger executives though he remained the team's president and later vice-chairman.[x] One of his final hands-on moves as an executive was drafting Paul Pierce in 1998. Pierce was the one player that kept the team afloat during the early 2000's.

Death and Legacy

Red Auerbach would hold on to his position as the Boston Celtics' head coach until 2006. While he had given most of the management duties to Danny Ainge, one of his former players in the 80's, he remained as a special consultant for some of the franchise's moves despite how he had diminished in health. He was often seen in a wheelchair due to heart problems.[iv]

On October 28, 2006, Red Auerbach's heart problems had finally taken their toll on him. He would suffer a heart attack that ultimately took his life on the same day. He was survived by his two daughters Nancy and Randy. The entire league mourned his death, and it was a consensus belief that he was one of the greatest people the NBA has ever seen.

Red Auerbach would die as arguably the greatest head coach in league history. At the time of his death, he had won nine titles as a head coach and seven rings as an executive for a total of 16 rings. Only Phil Jackson, who would later win ten championships during his stints as the head coach of the Chicago Bulls and the Los Angeles Lakers, would come close to his accomplishments concerning championships.

Chapter 3: What Made Red Auerbach a Great Leader

Wisdom

One of the reasons why Red Auerbach was an excellent leader for several decades, and not only when he was a head coach, was that he was such a wise person. It was his wisdom that helped him connect with his players and made him so knowledgeable about the ins and outs of what was happening both on and off the court. His experience as a teacher and basketball coach at an early stage in his life helped him become a wiser coach when he moved to the NBA.

Red Auerbach's words of wisdom always got into his players, and they have learned to follow the teachings that their head coach has bestowed. Auerbach always said, "If you get the talent, you gotta use it, and you better not lose it." Auerbach knew talent when he saw it. More importantly, he always preached to his players that talent is wasted when not used properly. Because of this, all the talented players he drafted were able to maximize whatever skills they had.

"Natural abilities are like natural plants; they need pruning by study." Those words come from English philosopher Francis Bacon. Red Auerbach learned how to live by those words. He would also preach those words to his players to teach them how crucial it was for people to learn how to study their abilities or else they would wither like plants. This was how his players learned how to hone their natural abilities and developed over time as capable contributors or even as All-Stars themselves.

Red Auerbach also stressed the importance of self-confidence and knowing how to trust others. He always wanted his players to be confident in themselves and to learn how to believe in what their teammates could do. Red often said, "He who believes in nobody knows that he himself is not to be trusted." This was one of the foundations of Red Auerbach's team basketball. None of his players were selfish to the point that they hogged all of the possessions and scoring opportunities. Instead, everyone on the team shared the ball as much as they could.

Finally, one of his most important words of wisdom was the foundation of his coaching success during the 60's. "Basketball is like war in that offensive weapons are developed first, and it always takes a while for the defense to catch up." It was because of this belief that Red Auerbach focused the importance of the fast break, which forced the tempo to speed up in favor of quick baskets before the defense could adjust at the other end. Because the rest of the NBA was not yet accustomed to a quick pace and running style of play, the Boston Celtics saw a lot of success early on before teams learned how to defend the fast break.

Red Auerbach's belief that offense is first developed and that defenses would take a while to adjust has been true not only during his time as a head coach but also throughout the history of the league. The NBA has always evolved to what the offense dictates instead of whatever looks the defense allows. Throughout different eras, the defense always adjusted to the offense.

During the 80's and 90's, the NBA saw an influx of isolation specialists. It took the NBA some time to adjust to the way players like Michael Jordan and Allen Iverson played because they also needed to change certain rules to allow the defense more leeway. And when dominant centers suddenly rose up during the 90's, it took a while for teams to adjust to how those big men played. Defenses would suddenly pack the paint to prevent those centers from dominating. And because players have grown to become so athletic, coaches would always preach their defenders to focus on protecting the basket and the lane from streaking superstars.

But during the second decade of the 2000's, athletic guards and great shooters suddenly became prevalent in the NBA. Coaches such as Steve Kerr, Gregg Popovich, and Mike D'Antoni have preached the importance of running to the three-point line in the corners and wings in transition instead of streaking towards the basket like the teams of old used to do. Defenses were initially confused about such a tactic and would still try to protect the basket instead of the more dangerous but less efficient three-point line.

Not only did coaches try to preach the importance of running towards the three-point line but they also went back to Auerbach's basic tactics of ball movement. While defenses adjusted to the isolation styles of players such as Kobe Bryant, LeBron James, Carmelo Anthony, and Kevin Durant, Steve Kerr, and Gregg Popovich preached ball movement instead of simply allowing one or two players to take over and create for others.

Because defenses were yet to learn how to defend quick ball and player movement and three-point shooting, both Kerr and Popovich won championships because their teams' offense evolved before defensive tactics could adjust. And if you trace everything, it goes back to how Red Auerbach was ahead of his time when he believed that developing a new offensive system would mean that defenses would have to adjust later.

Leadership Tree

When he was coaching the Boston Celtics, one of Red Auerbach's fundamental beliefs was that a great leader would always create more leaders that would follow him. It was this belief that made him an effective leader on his own. It was the fact that several other players learned how to become leaders under him that proved that Auerbach could preach his beliefs and philosophies and that his players and his protégés were willing to follow in his footsteps.

Red Auerbach produced leaders and championship coaches such as Bill Russell, Tom Heinsohn, KC Jones, and Bill Sharman.[xi] Russell won two titles as the head coach that succeeded Auerbach in Boston. Tom Heinsohn would also win two championships later in the 70's. Meanwhile, Bill Sharman won the Lakers' first title in Los Angeles in 1972 after winning the ABA championship with the Utah Stars. KC Jones worked under Sharman in Los Angeles as an assistant when the latter won the 1972 championship. He then led the Big Three era of the Celtics to two titles in the 80's.

But how could he produce a coaching and leadership tree that became as successful as he was? First and foremost, Red Auerbach was a teacher before he became an NBA coach. He knew the importance of motivating his players and knowing what motivated them to not only become better players but leaders themselves. Red empowered his players to become leaders by allowing them to flourish not only as on-court leaders but also as locker room voices.

The way Red Auerbach built the Boston Celtics' dynasty also proved that the winning tradition would not end with him. He developed ordinary players into superstars and superstars into leaders. Because of this, winning became a tradition in Boston, and he always made sure that anyone that followed after him was just as motivated as he was when it came to winning games and championships.

And when he became an executive, Red Auerbach also made sure the players he drafted and coaches he hired had the makings of great leaders themselves. Larry Bird turned out to become an excellent coach in Indiana even though he failed to win a title. He also became successful as an executive. Another one of his former players, Danny Ainge, followed him as the Celtics' executive. Ainge was the orchestrator of the moves that brought Kevin Garnett and Ray Allen to Boston to win the 2008 championship, the first title the Celtics won since 1986.

Even after he retired from coaching in 1966, Red Auerbach's influence reached all the way to 2008, two years after he passed away. He always had a hand in the Boston Celtics' success no matter what era it was. It was either because he was the one that drafted the players that led the Celtics on the court or because he was the one that hired the coach and executive, who were usually one of his former players. Almost no other leader in league history has had a hand in his team's success for as long as Red Auerbach has. It was all because he made sure he created leaders as capable as he was.

Great Motivator

In Bill Russell's book, *Second Wind*, he said that Red Auerbach was indeed a genius of a coach, but his greatest skill as a leader was that he was a master motivator that knew that there were a lot of different ways to psyche people up.[xii] Russell described him as a person that knew how many different personalities there are and that it took different methods to motivate those different personalities.

Red Auerbach knew that everyone responded differently to certain tactics of motivation. He used different ways to motivate different players because of how much they varied in personalities. For instance, Auerbach yelled at players such as Tom Sanders and Don Nelson more often than not because they responded well when they were scolded unlike the other guys on the team.

However, Red Auerbach rarely yelled at his best player, Bill Russell. Auerbach even had to go through the process of asking permission from Russell to yell at him in future practices. Red only did that when he felt like the team needed it. The weirdest part was that Bill Russell did not always comply whenever Red Auerbach wanted to yell at him.[xi]

Russell noted in *Second Wind* that Red Auerbach had different motivational tactics when dealing with different players. With Tom Heinsohn, he had to yell at him personally and frequently because that was what it took to get him to work harder. For Tom Sanders and Don Nelson, Red would bully them in a different way than he did with Heinsohn. However, it was an entirely different case for KC Jones. For Jones, Auerbach only had to talk to him honestly and leave him alone because he knew that the guard could already pick the message up without yelling at him.[xi]

Red Auerbach did not always ask his players what motivated them the best. Instead, it was a process of trial and error and a lot of observation. Red, of course, had to yell, recognize, compliment, or drive his players hard to see if they responded to different motivational tactics. Described by Russell as a good psychologist, Auerbach understood his players' psyche and observed a lot to see what it took to motivate them to become better players.[xi]

As an example, Bill Russell once told a story during his rookie season when he was standing out of place while Bob Cousy and Bill Sharman were both posting their men on the low post. When Red asked him what was wrong, Russell told him in disgust that everybody wanted to play center out there and it was not his place to tell them not to. While other coaches might have seen this as an insult to their authority, Auerbach did not impose himself on the rookie center.

As a black man that lived at a time when there were still differences in rights between African-Americans and whites, Bill Russell would not have responded well to a white authoritarian figure that scolded and told him what to do. Instead, he told every other player on the team that nobody else would play center except Bill. He also, later on, allowed Russell to get off the floor to block shots instead of forcing him to keep his feet on the ground to defend by contesting shots, which was what Auerbach preferred. He allowed Russell to be himself as a way of motivating him rather than scolding and screaming at him like he did with the other players.[xiv]

Red Auerbach also used pride as one of his primary ways to get his team motivated. He wanted his players to see how great it was to be excellent. It was the pride of being winners that he used to get them going. He would always tell his guys that they were better off spending the summer as champions and members of the most excellent team in basketball than sulking at home without a championship ring.

Bill Russell would also say that Red Auerbach never did the same thing twice. Since ways of motivation often change, Red did not do the same tactic over and over again even though he knew it worked in the past. He had to mix things up and find new ways to motivate his players, who were growingly more difficult to motivate because they were winning titles every season. As they say, it is always more difficult to motivate someone to stay at the top than a person who wants to reach the top.

Russell said that Red had to dream of different ways to get the team fired up and get his message across. While Auerbach was a person that could think of a lot of different ways to get his players more focused on winning, his greatest skill was that he could use those same reasons on different players while knowing who those reasons best applied to and when to use them reasons at the right time.[xi]

Red Auerbach would also pass his ability to motivate players to some of the coaches he handpicked. One such coach was Dave Cowens, who was the team's best center during the 70's. Cowens used motivation as one of his primary weapons in trying to reform what was then a struggling Celtics franchise during the tail end of the 70's era. One of his ways of motivating his players were one-on-one contests that involved a cash prize. And when they were on the road, Dave Cowens also gave up his hotel suite and had his players vote on who got to use that room.[xiii] Those were things he learned from Red Auerbach himself.

Because motivation is best described as a moving target, Red Auerbach had to innovate new ways to get his players psyched up to win games even though they had so little incentive to win after winning title after title each season. He knew that he would not yield the same results if he did things the same way every time. If he did that, he would not have won nine titles in ten years. But Auerbach used different methods in every one of those nine titles. Motivation is always vital to winning, and Auerbach proved that during his stint as a head coach.

Player Empowerment

One of the many lasting images of Red Auerbach that people have in their minds is the authoritarian version of himself—the man that would scream in the faces of referees and opposing star players to the tune of an unprecedented amount of ejections and technical fouls. In some other minds, he was the cigar-smoking head coach that smoked after a big victory or before he gave officials a piece of his mind. And for outsiders that saw him in practices and games, he was the coach that would scold his players whenever they were out of focus. However, Red was more than any of that to his players that loved playing under him.

For his players such as Bill Russell, Red Auerbach was more of a calm and calculating leader that treated his players not so different from another legendary coach such as Phil Jackson. Auerbach was always seen in contrast to Jackson, who would later surpass his nine championships with ten of his own. Phil was often seen as a calm coach that allowed his players a lot of leeway on the floor. He almost never screamed at officials or scolded his players. However, Red was often seen as the opposite because of how hot-headed he was to some people.

But Russell always thought that Auerbach was not the opposite of Jackson. Red was the type of coach that allowed his players a lot of freedom on the floor. He gave them the authority to add new tactics and also allowed them to change strategies in the middle of the game. And according to Russell, he almost never scolded his guys after losses because Red Auerbach knew that his words would not work on players that were already down on themselves. He also believed that his guys already believed that they knew what went wrong and what they had to improve.[xiv]

Red Auerbach empowered his players to know what to do out on the floor and to adjust to whatever plays and difficulties they were put into by their opponents. In a lot of ways, he was Phil Jackson even before the man called the "Zen Master" was coaching in the NBA. He allowed them to correct their wrongs and steer the ship back on course without having to scold them.

Auerbach once said that he took exception with teams that demanded loyalty from their players but gave little in return. As a way of empowering his players, he was loyal and trusting towards his players as much as he demanded his players to be loyal and trusting towards him and the system. It was always a two-way street for Red Auerbach.

His role was to look after his players as long as they gave their all to the goal of winning a title.[xv]

The way he empowered his players led to them being excellent leaders of their own. Bill Russell, Bill Sharman, Tom Heinsohn, KC Jones, and Dave Cowens, among others, have gone on to become fantastic coaches after learning a great deal from Red Auerbach and after becoming empowered early because they were players for the Boston Celtics.

Oversight

While some would say that the tendency for oversight or unintentionally seeing something puts a person at a disadvantage, it was not the same for Red Auerbach as a leader. Auerbach's tendency for oversight was best applied to how he never saw a player's color, reputation, statistics, or attitude. What was crucial for Red was that his players were motivated and that they contributed to a winning final score at the end of a game.[xv]

In 1950, Red Auerbach made history when he drafted Chuck Cooper, who would go on to become the first

African-American player in the NBA. When asked about his decision to draft Cooper, Red dismissed the issue and said that he thought that a player's color was an oversight in his case because he never cared whether the guy was black or white as long as he could contribute to the team and was motivated to win.

As time went on, Red Auerbach continued to draft and add black players to the Boston Celtics, claiming that he never thought about their color but only what they could do on the floor. Such players included Bill Russell, KC Jones, Sam Jones, and Tom Sanders. Considered as a colorblind coach, Auerbach was more focused on skill, talent, potential, and ability rather than color or race.

In 1964, Red Auerbach would field the league's first starting five composed of all black players. Those five players were Bill Russell, Tom Sanders, Sam Jones, KC Jones, and Willie Naulls. Decades later, players of color became a norm in the NBA, and most teams now field starting fives composed of African-Americans. There are even teams that are all African-Americans.

When Red Auerbach decided to give up his role as a head coach in 1966, the first decision he made as the Boston Celtics' general manager was to appoint Bill Russell as the new coach of the team without hesitation. Russell would become the first African-American head coach in NBA history and the first in all four of America's major professional sports. He blazed the trail for black players and coaches in the NBA to the point that African-American stars and personnel have even dominated the league today. It has become a norm not only in basketball but the entire country as well.

Another example of how Red Auerbach always overlooked a players' color was when he formed a Boston Celtics team in the 80's that was dominantly white.[xvi] People criticized the makeup of the Celtics as "too white" in a league that was increasingly becoming dominated by bigger, stronger, and more athletic black players. But Auerbach did not see his team as white or black. Instead, he saw a group of players that were hardworking and had skill and talents that fit the Celtics' winning tradition. The result was three NBA championships for the Boston Celtics that decade.

Red Auerbach not only overlooked a person's race and color but also their statistics. As one of the first coaches that advocated a team that had a balanced attack and with players that specialized in different roles, whether they were starters or were playing off the bench, Auerbach's focus was fielding the five players that were in the best position to win him games and not necessarily the best five players he had on the team.[xvii]

Red Auerbach often said that one of the biggest mistakes that coaches made was that they used their best players instead of the ones that could help them win. For him, what was most important was picking players that could help balance out the team because there was only one ball, not five. That was the reason why Red Auerbach often fielded a team of players that had specific roles.

During the late 50's and 60's, Auerbach's team was composed of specialists. Bill Russell was their rebounder and paint defender. He rarely scored the ball. Bob Cousy was the team's facilitator, especially on the break. Sam Jones, Bill Sharman, and KC Jones were there to score from the perimeter and finish transition plays. Meanwhile,

Frank Ramsey and John Havlicek were the Celtics' sixth men in different eras and never cared whether they started or contributed off the bench. And while most teams focused on their superstars and five best players while giving them 40 minutes a night, only Bill Russell consistently averaged more than 40 minutes per game while the other players barely played over 30.

Auerbach also often had players that had more ability, talent, and skill than his other guys but were mostly too stubborn and selfish to play a definite role on the team. Those were guys that did not last long in Boston. He always remarked at how older players and ones with less ability could more easily understand that they were on the team to specialize in one role than those that had a lot of skill and talent but were too engrossed with their playing time and possessions.[xvii] This was why guys such as Bob Brannum, Clyde Lovellette, and Jim Loscutoff had jobs and roles under Red Auerbach while talented players such as Ramsey and Havlicek accepted their role as the best players off the bench. Frank Ramsey is widely considered as the NBA's first sixth man while Havlicek was one of his first successors.

Because of how Red Auerbach was more focused on his team's balance and how everyone played a defined role on the team, he always overlooked his players' statistics. Saying, "I go by what I see," Red measured the worth of a player based on how they performed on the floor instead of what the stat sheet showed. He said that stats would only interest him when they started to show and measure how much fortitude and hard work a player had. But, to this day, they hardly measure how hard a player works on the floor and how well he comes through in the most important situations of a game.

There was even an instance during the 80's when Bill Walton was the sixth man off the bench, where Red Auerbach noticed how unhappy the former MVP center was. Walton told him that he felt like he was not contributing to the team because he was not scoring. Red dismissed that thought and told Walton that he did not care about scoring as long as he was rolling, playing defense, and running the floor hard. Bill Walton was surprised at the notion that Auerbach never cared that he was not scoring. What was important to the Celtic's great leader was that his players were contributing by doing their roles.

What was most crucial to Auerbach was how a player performed on the floor on the basis of what he saw instead of how many points, rebounds, and assists the statistics showed. A guy could have a triple-double or average 30 points and 20 rebounds a night but would, however, take bad shots, leave opponents on the defensive end, and fail to run hard. For Red, statistics did not mean much if a player failed to cover the parts of the game that statistics cannot measure.[xvii] And if a player had monster stats but did not perform as well in the intangibles of the game, the result would most likely not favor his team.

Red Auerbach's tendency to overlook things also reflected in how he made deals. He said that teams offered him plenty of trade deals that would have given him a player with more talent and star power than he would lose. However, he almost always turned those trades down because of how much he valued team chemistry. A player may have all the talent in the world, but such acquisition would go to waste if he did not mesh well with the guys that Red already had on the team.

Despite how much Red Auerbach overlooked a lot of things such as race, color, and statistics, he never failed to look at the things that mattered. He only believed in what his eyes were telling him and not what skin color and numbers were showing him. He focused on what was happening on the floor instead of what the media and statistics were telling the world. That was what oversight meant for Red Auerbach, a head coach that loved to ignore the things that did not matter but always looked at the intangibles that helped his team reach their goal of winning a championship.

Genius

When you look at it simply, the reason why Red Auerbach was a great leader was that he was a genius. Red's genius transcended the realm of basketball and sports. He was an excellent on-court strategist, revolutionary offensive and defensive guru, expert at psychological warfare, a master at scouting hidden talent, and talented manager.

Red Auerbach's genius showed in every facet of his job as both the head coach and general manager of the Boston Celtics. One of the many ways he displayed his great strategic genius was when he revolutionized the Celtics' offense. At that time, players liked to play the game slowly and milked the clock at every possession to try to decrease the opponents' scoring opportunities. However, Auerbach had other plans. He would try to speed the game up at every possible opportunity by making his players run the fast break as defenses tried to get back on the other end of the floor. And when the league introduced the 24-second shot clock in the middle of the 50's, Auerbach's quick scoring strategy worked to perfection because teams were now inclined to take a shot before the buzzer sounded.

While anyone would describe Red Auerbach as a fiery hothead because of how he showed his emotions during games by screaming at officials, opposing players, and even team owners, some would go on to say that the on-court antics were merely to make the Boston Celtics an even better team. No matter how many cigars he smoked or how many times he had to leave the floor because of his tirades, it simply benefitted the Celtics.

Red Auerbach designed his colorful on-court antics and habits as a way to not only make the game more colorful but also to intimidate referees and officials and to get opposing coaches and owners' focus on the game at hand or the happenings that were more important.[xiv] And when he was smoking cigars or getting his team fired up by fighting for them by screaming at referees and getting thrown out of the game, the crowd only got wilder. By playing at the edge of the rules, Auerbach became an adored figure in Boston, and the team only became more popular in the New England area because Red made it more fun and exciting to watch the Celtics' games.

Mastering the art of psychological warfare was also part of Red Auerbach's genius. When the Boston Celtics were against a team that had a high scorer, Red preached to his defenders to tell the other guys on the opposing squad that they were useful because their best player takes all the shots. This got the opponents' role players' minds out of the game because they would constantly ponder about how useful they were.

The way Red Auerbach scouted talented players and weaved his way to get the best players of the draft also showed how much of a genius he was. One of the greatest stories in basketball history was how Red acquired Bill Russell in the 1956 NBA Draft. It was a move that not only changed the fate of the Boston Celtics but also created a massive shift of power in the NBA.

Bill Russell was not the best player coming out of high school, unlike his eternal rival Wilt Chamberlain. However, when Russell finished college, he had already won the NCAA title twice and was arguably the best prospect of the class of 1956 because of his massive defensive presence and unparalleled rebounding abilities. Red Auerbach wanted a player of his caliber and knew that Russell was going to be the missing piece of what would become a championship team for years to come.

Red Auerbach would trade proven big man Ed Macauley and the seventh pick of the draft to the St. Louis Hawks in exchange for the second overall pick. But Red was not finished. He still had to deal with the fact that the Rochester Royals, the predecessors of what is known as the Sacramento Kings today, had the top overall pick in 1956. They had no reason not to draft Russell, but Auerbach offered them a deal they could not refuse.

Boston Celtics owner Walter A. Brown was the president of a traveling show called the Ice Capades. Back then, basketball was not the most lucrative sport in America and shows like the Ice Capades were much more profitable. And with the blessing of Brown, Red Auerbach convinced the Rochester Royals to stay away from Bill Russell by offering the Ice Capades to them for free. Red would eventually draft the biggest piece of the team that would win nine championships for the Boston Celtics with something as simple as offering a show to the Royals.

After Bill Russell retired from the NBA, the Celtics needed another big man to protect the paint. Red Auerbach revealed in his autobiography titled *On and Off the Court* that he was able to swindle the relatively unknown Dave Cowens of FSU from any other team when he scouted him once. When Red went on to watch an FSU game to look at Cowens, he would leave as early as halftime looking like he was not interested in the big man. Because of that, nobody else wanted Dave Cowens out of the belief that Red Auerbach did not think he was someone special. But it was all a ruse, and he would draft Cowens, who would go on to win two titles for the team in the 70's.

Another of his genius moves was when he drafted Larry Bird in 1978. Because Larry Legend was a transferee and still had one more year left in college, he wanted to finish his degree but was already eligible to be drafted in 1978. Red Auerbach was interested in Bird, but he was still a relative unknown except for the Boston Celtics' general manager and the Indiana Pacers, who always got to see Larry play at Indiana State University.

But when Bird spoke with the Pacers, he told them that he wanted to stay in college one more year to finish his studies. Wanting a player that could help the team right away, Indiana opted to pass on the future legend. Since the next few teams were unaware of how good Bird was before he led ISU to a 33-1 record in the 1978-79 season, he went undrafted until the Boston Celtics took him. Auerbach took advantage of the opportunity despite knowing Bird was not available the following season and despite other teams criticizing their pick. But that was not the genius move that would make the Celtics the best Eastern team in the 80's.

In 1980, Red Auerbach made what is arguably considered the best move he has ever made as a general manager. Dubbed as "The Steal of the Century," he formed what would become the Boston Celtics' original Big Three with one simple move. He had long coveted the Golden State Warriors' star center Robert Parish because he wanted a center that could man the paint for the Celtics. He also wanted to draft Kevin McHale and was in the best position to draft him because Boston had the top overall pick of 1980.

But instead of drafting McHale out of Minnesota just like that, he used the top overall pick as leverage to complete the Boston Celtics' championship team. Red Auerbach would trade the top overall pick and the seventh pick to the Golden State Warriors in exchange for Parish and the third draft pick. Since the Warriors needed a center, they took

Joe Barry Carroll, who was college basketball's best at that position. The Utah Jazz, needing a guard, would choose Darrell Griffith with their second overall pick. The Celtics were then in a position to draft Kevin McHale with the third overall draft choice.

Acquiring McHale and Parish in the same year completed what was to become the Celtics' Big Three star frontline. Bird, McHale, and Parish would eventually become Hall of Famers and would lead the Boston Celtics to three championships during the 80's thanks to how Red Auerbach was able to execute such moves to acquire them and to how he surrounded them with complementary role players.

In 2017, one his former players, Danny Ainge, the general manager of the Celtics at that time, made a move similar to what Red Auerbach did in 1980. The Celtics owned the first overall draft pick of that class and looked to bolster the team by using it as leverage. Since the consensus top choice was Markelle Fultz, a point guard, the Boston Celtics had no incentive to draft him because they already had a logjam at that position. What the Celtics needed was a wing player to complete what was considered a championship-contending roster.

Danny Ainge would use the Philadelphia 76ers need of a point guard to his advantage. He would trade the top overall pick to Philadelphia in exchange for the 76ers' third pick and another future first-round pick. Boston would draft Jayson Tatum, the player they wanted in the first place, with the third pick while also getting something in return for the future with the first-round draft pick they got from the 76ers, who drafted Markelle Fultz. It was a classic move straight out of Red Auerbach's playbook.

As much of a genius as Red Auerbach was in the world of basketball, he understood the ins and outs of management just as well. He always considered loyalty as one of the more critical factors of managing an organization. However, one thing about loyalty that most organizations were unaware of or were refusing to accept was that it was a two-way street.

Red Auerbach always considered trust and loyalty as a two-way street that required both the organization and the player or employee to give and take on almost equal terms. Auerbach was aware that most businesses demand loyalty from their employees without considering that they should also be loyal to them as well. But Auerbach ran the Celtics differently.

As one of the best organizations in the NBA since the league's inception, the Boston Celtics have always been a franchise that cared about its players and employees because of how Red Auerbach laid the foundations. Red built a Boston Celtics organization that cared about the players but still made good moves that made the team profitable and competitive.[xviii]

Genius managers know that they also need to take care of their personnel long after they have moved on from their playing years. Most of Red Auerbach's players retired without any pressure from the organization because they knew that they did a good job and it was time to move on from being a player.[xviii] Auerbach helped them transition to life after basketball by hiring the guys he helped develop from the ground up to keep them within the organization and make the franchise more stable instead of letting them move on from the team.

Red Auerbach also understood what it meant for his players to be happy just as any other employee in a company would want to enjoy his working environment. He did not want his personnel to work with fear because he realized that he could not get the best out of his players through those means. Players and employees that work under fear are not as innovative as the ones that enjoy what they do because their only focus is on keeping the boss happy and staying out of trouble as much as they can. However, people that enjoy their jobs do not fear messing up or getting into trouble as long as ingenuity in the workplace is allowed.

But this did not mean that Red did not have rules and disciplinary procedures. The Celtics had rules that they wanted their players and personnel to follow as much as any other organization. However, the difference was in how Auerbach enforced these rules. He never threatened his guys or fined them for any trouble they might get into or any rules they might break. Instead, they talked some sense into them and tempered the employees with understanding.[xviii]

And while Auerbach knows that a well-paid employee is a happy employee, he never pays the player more than his value was to the team. He was willing to give his guys a high salary but not beyond what they were contributing to the organization. Running a basketball team was just like any other business. Being the genius that he was, Red Auerbach was aware of the parallelisms between the two and built the franchise the same way as any other successful businessman would build a large company.

But Red Auerbach was also aware that he was not a perfect businessman. He might have been a genius manager for the Boston Celtics, but he thought that he did not have the knowledge or tools to manage organizations such as the Red Sox or the Patriots, as some newspapers during that time suggested. Auerbach knew that what he needed to become a great manager was knowledge of the product.[xviii] For instance, you could not sell a car without knowing the specifications.

Knowledge of the product was part of what made Red Auerbach a genius manager and coach in basketball. He paid his dues by being the man that had to coach, scout opposing teams and college players, organize practices, and maintain discipline on the team all by himself. It was that experience that helped him gain the knowledge he needed to know the product. And the moment he gained enough knowledge of the product, he perfected it and made managing a basketball organization his craft. His genius in that regard was unmatched even until the day he died.

Chapter 4: How Red Auerbach Maximized Player Potential

Teamwork

The basic foundation of how Red Auerbach could produce quality players and make stars out relative unknowns and excellent contributors out of hard-workers was how he emphasized the importance of teamwork to the Boston Celtics. Teamwork was a concept that was rare back then when teams stressed the importance of relying on superstars.

Back then, the formula to win basketball games was simple: allow your superstars to take over. The concept was to give the ball down low to Wilt Chamberlain. Some would let Paul Arizin shoot his way to high-scoring games. Another way was to make Oscar Robertson create for the team or himself. And some would give room for Elgin Baylor to dominate games. However, that was not what Red Auerbach's teams were all about.

Red Auerbach was able to get the most out of his players because he allowed them to play as a team instead of relying on just one or two superstars. He did not rely only on his superstars such as Bob Cousy, Bill Sharman, or Bill Russell, who could all put up 30 points a night if they wanted to. Instead, he emphasized the importance of moving the ball around and letting others contribute and produce in their own way.

Red Auerbach was known as a coach that never cared about his players' statistics, and only one stat mattered to him. What was important to him was that the number of points his team scored was greater than how many the opposing team had. That was the simple key to winning basketball games, and Auerbach believed that the best way to achieve it was to play as a team.

While statistics did not matter much for Red, they showed how well his Boston Celtics played as a team. The 1956-57 Boston Celtics, who were the first to win a title for the franchise, had six players scoring in double digits. The leading scorer was Bill Sharman, who was followed by Bob Cousy. Neither one of them finished in the top five in scoring. Despite how good those two veterans were, Red's best player was the rookie Bill Russell, who could have dominated everyone else in the paint had he been told to. Instead, Auerbach let his team move the ball around and emphasized how crucial it was to let others contribute as well.

That 1956-57 team also featured Rookie of the Year Tom Heinsohn, who produced for the Celtics instantly because of how Red Auerbach allowed everyone to flourish under his system. That roster also had Frank Ramsey, a guard off the bench. Despite barely starting any games, Ramsey would produce well for the Celtics in limited minutes and would earn the tag as the first sixth man in the history of the NBA. He would remain the league's premier sixth man for years to come under Red Auerbach.

The epitome of teamwork was the 1962-63 version of the Boston Celtics. That team had a total of seven players that could pour in double digits in scoring. Not one of their players could score over 20 points a night because no one cared who was scoring as long as the team won at the end of the night. Bill Russell, Sam Jones, Tom Sanders, Bob

Cousy, Tom Heinsohn, Frank Ramsey, and John Havlicek all scored in double digits. Two players from the bench, namely Ramsey and the rookie Havlicek, also scored in double digits. Havlicek would follow in Ramsey's footsteps as the league's premier bench scorer.

The beauty of that 1962-63 team was that Red Auerbach spread the minutes across the board. Everyone had an equal opportunity to contribute. His roster was 11 men deep. Auerbach had eight players averaging at least 20 minutes a night. Among those eight players, only Bill Russell and Sam Jones averaged more than 30 minutes per game. Their teamwork was truly a sight to behold, and the Boston Celtics' players were contributing well despite not playing the same amount of minutes as some of the league's best stars.

Because Red Auerbach allowed teamwork to flourish on his teams, his individual players were able to maximize their potential. While other strong players were hidden deep in the bench or playing in the shadow of dominant superstars on other teams, Auerbach realized that everyone could contribute. More importantly, he allowed them to do so by giving them the chance and minutes. This was what made the Boston Celtics the most balanced team under Red Auerbach. And for Red, balance was a direct product of teamwork.

Playing a Role

Everybody on Red Auerbach's team was inclined to work as a single unit. Teamwork was the reason behind how they were able to win championships under Auerbach's leadership as a coach nine times in ten years. However, a critical factor to how they were able to function well as a team was balance. The Boston Celtics' championship teams were so balanced because everybody on the floor played a defined role.

Red Auerbach was one of the revolutionary figures of contributors that we now call "role players." The Boston Celtics teams under Auerbach had players that were merely on the team because they had roles to play and not because they could do everything that a basketball star could do. At a time when the league placed a premium on players that were capable of doing everything, Red Auerbach focused more on spreading contributions out and having his players specialize in the roles they were best at.

Back then, stars such as Paul Arizin, Elgin Baylor, Wilt Chamberlain, and Oscar Robertson had to do everything. Arizin was a fantastic scorer and rebounder. Baylor practically led the team in scoring, rebounding, and passing. After averaging a triple-double and flirting with the stat every single night, Robertson was your quintessential do-everything guy. And for Chamberlain, he carried the load every game. He was averaging 48 minutes a night while putting up 40 to 50 points and 20 to 25 rebounds while also blocking the sun out with his ability to defend the basket at the highest level possible. It was an era where stars had to do everything for the team and when coaches expected those stars to go out and contribute in every facet of the game.

Red Auerbach coached differently and was ahead of his time in that regard. Teamwork was prevalent, nobody had to do everything, and no one hogged the possessions or spotlight. Everyone on that team had a role to play, and nobody was asked to do everything on his own. The heavy lifting was everyone's load to carry and was not just the burden of one or two superstars.

Bill Russell was always Red Auerbach's best player, but he never had to carry the team all by himself. While he was as huge and athletic as any other center in the league and might have even been more dominant than 90% of the other big men in the league, he did not have to do what Wilt Chamberlain was asked to do. Wilt had to score 30 to 50 points, rebound 20 misses, block shots by the dozen, and make plays for others all while he was playing every minute of the game. However, Russell was merely asked to focus on the two roles he was best at.

Red Auerbach's role for Bill Russell was to have his center defend the basket and contest shots near the rim. He shrank the floor and forced opposing players to shoot tough perimeter shots instead of the easier layups near the basket. And after forcing those tough shots, the team left him alone to grab rebounds. Russell never averaged less than 18 rebounds his entire career and has a career rebounding average of 22.5 because Auerbach had him focus on grabbing misses after he forced his opponents to put up tough shots. He was averaging more rebounds than points throughout his career and every season even though he had enough skill and power in him to put up 20 to 30 points a night. But as unselfish as Russell was, the points did not matter to him, and he would instead focus on defense, rebounding, and throwing outlet passes to streaking scorers.

Bill Russell was not the only player that complied with what his role was. Bob Cousy, considered as the league's first superstar point guard, was known for his flashy dribbling and creative passing. With ball-handling skills that were unmatched and a shooting stroke that was one of the best at that time, he could have been one of the premier scorers and do-it-all players in the NBA. However, Cousy's role under Auerbach was to orchestrate the plays and make life easy for others. He was the first target of outlet passes because he ran the floor hard to either score on the fast break or find open teammates on the dead run.

Shooting guard Bill Sharman also had a specific role on the team. He never had to create shots for himself because he was a target for Russell and Cousy on transition plays. He was also one of the first premier shooters in the NBA. Sam

Jones would later inherit that role as an efficient shooting guard that played within the flow of the game.

Meanwhile, there were players whose best contributions were not tangible on paper and would have to be seen by the naked eye to be evaluated well. Tom Heinsohn, an All-Star that could put up good statistics, was better known not for his skills but his hustle and energy. He was the quintessential workhorse for the Boston Celtics. He was also someone of supreme confidence, and all the shots he took were good for him. And when he got into broadcasting, Heinsohn would be best known for putting high praise on players that loved to hustle as much as he did back in the day.

Red Auerbach was also well-known for revolutionizing what we now call the sixth man. Knowing how crucial it was to have a strong and balanced bench that could put up points when starters were resting and overwhelming the opposing team with their fresh legs, Red placed emphasis on empowering his second unit. It was always led by what he called the sixth man.

The sixth man is a player that almost never starts a game but plays the same amount of minutes as a starter and can produce just as well or even better than his starting counterparts. At a time when coaches placed a lot of emphasis on star players and starting units by having them play 40 minutes a night, the sixth man was a revolutionary role because it allowed the team to stay competitive even when the bench was on the floor. And when bench players are empowered and producing well, starters are allowed more rest to prevent fatigue and injuries. Red used this to his advantage by giving a good amount of minutes to his bench players, who were led by a sixth man.

Red Auerbach always had players that were comfortable playing a role off the bench as the best player of the second unit. Frank Ramsey was his first sixth man and is widely considered the first of his kind in league history. Ramsey would pass the torch down to rookie John Havlicek during the 1962-63 season, which was his final year in the league. Both Ramsey and Havlicek played heavy minutes off the bench for the Celtics during that season because Boston had one of the deepest benches in league history.

Players such as Ramsey and Havlicek paved the way for what is now called the Sixth Man of the Year award. The inaugural award was presented to Bobby Jones in 1983. But if there was such an award back then when Ramsey and Havlicek played, they would have certainly won the award multiple times. Nevertheless, three of Red Auerbach's handpicked players, when he was a general manager in the 80's, would become winners of that award. Kevin McHale won it twice in a row in 1984 and '85 while Bill Walton would win the award after him in 1986.

The sixth man was a role that Red Auerbach could not do without when he was a coach and general manager. He always wanted someone with star quality leading the second unit. Of course, that player had to be unselfish and comfortable playing off the bench instead of starting. The sixth man became empowered because he was the star of his own unit. It was like he was leading his own team off the bench rather than becoming just one of the guys in the starting unit. Such a role has become a norm in today's NBA as Red Auerbach was already ahead of his time back in the 50's and 60's.

Even older players could contribute for Red Auerbach. Guys like Jim Loscutoff and Clyde Lovellette were some of Auerbach's favorite players not because they were skilled and talented but because they were willing to accept their roles and specialize in certain aspects of the game. Red once said that he preferred older veterans to young and talented players because they always understood what it meant to accept a role.[xvii] What use was there for the best player in the league if he was not willing to accept the role given to him?

Giving specific roles to unselfish but skilled players was how Red Auerbach empowered some of his players and allowed them to maximize their potential. If everyone was just ordered to watch what the best players on the team were doing while doing the smaller jobs such as occasional scoring and rebounding, then those players could not contribute to the best of what their potential could have allowed them to do. But in Red Auerbach's Celtics' case, he knew the skills that his players were best at and allowed them to flourish by assigning them roles suitable for those skills. While not everyone became stars, certain players became specialists in their roles and were able to contribute well to how the Red's Celtics dominated that era.

Motivating Players

It is often said that teamwork only becomes possible once every employee or player begins to take responsibility for their actions and becomes accountable for their mistakes. In a common business setting, a leader is responsible for the team's overall performance. However, the leader is not always responsible for how willing his representatives and employees are to improve their performance.[xix]

Some managers and leaders often waste time trying to develop the wrong people. By wrong people, we mean those that are not willing to take action and responsibility for their well-being and self-improvement. These are the type of people that are not willing to change and improve to yield better results than they did before. So the basic principle, in this case, is to find people who desire to become better. Only those that desire to improve develop into better workers, employees, and players.[xix]

The desire to become better has always been the key factor in determining the outcome of how much a business or an entire organization could improve. If a player or employee does not have the desire to improve, any coaching, preaching, or mentoring is deemed useless in the long run. Desire has always been the most crucial part of improvement. The job of a coach or a leader is to be there to help his employees or players in their endeavor. However, everything else boils down to how much work the person is willing to put in to improve his performance.

With that said, Red Auerbach knew that he wanted to draft or sign players that had the desire within themselves to become great and become winners every year. The most critical part of it all was getting personnel that desired change and improvement. All he had to do was become a mentor to stir and bring out what best motivated a player to improve. And once Red did that, the only thing he needed to do was wait and see the results that his players were going to yield.

Bill Russell once said that Red Auerbach's greatest skill was not that he was a genius or that he had a lot of tricks up his sleeve. It was that he was a great motivator. Motivation was one way that Red got the most out of his players and how he got them to work hard every night. It was something that kept them going even after they won championship trophy after championship trophy each year.[xiv]

Red Auerbach, of course, had all kinds of ways to motivate his players to work harder depending on what type of personality or history the person had. For example, he did not act like an authoritative white figure that would have alarmed an African-American such as Bill Russell. Instead, he was a nurturing father to Russell whereas he was going hard on the other players such as Don Nelson and Tom Sanders. He also used a different approach to KC Jones, who he knew was smart enough to get the message without having to yell at him.[xiv]

In essence, Red Auerbach first had to get to know his players. A good leader would always want to know his personnel and employees better because everyone responds differently to how you approach them. For Red, he was well aware of the fact that his players had different personalities and histories. He had to change his approach depending on how a certain player reacted to how he tried to motivate him. Auerbach was not trying to be an authoritative figure but was also a father that tried to understand and learn about his players' personalities, traits, and tendencies. This was what made him the quintessential motivator of his time.

Of course, Red Auerbach also had to innovate his ways to motivate his players. Once a certain employee or player reaches the pinnacle of success, it becomes even more difficult to motivate them to perform better and to make them stay at the top. Because of that, Red had to change the way he motivated his players every season. It was a never-ending cycle of trying to make them see the effects of how much they could contribute to a championship run just by staying motivated.

While Red Auerbach may have employed different means to get his players pumped up and motivated to win a title and improve even after becoming champions, pride was his best tool. Convincing his players how great it was to become proud of themselves as part of the best basketball team in the world at the end of it all and during the offseason was what he used best to keep his guys motivated. Of course, the only way to become part of the best basketball team was to win a championship. And to win a championship, the players must stay motivated and try to become better to stay at the top of the mountain.

A leader, manager, mentor, or coach can only do so much to keep his players motivated and maximize their potential. But in Red Auerbach's case, he never failed to do his end in trying to convince his players to become better players themselves. Maximizing a person's potential has always been a two-way street. For the leader or coach, he only has to find what makes the person's desire tick and to be there whenever he was needed. But the player also has to put in the necessary work. And being the great leader and motivator that he was, Red Auerbach always made that two-way street work. The result was nine championship trophies and several Hall of Fame players and coaches that developed under his wing.

Chapter 5: Red Auerbach's System

Offense: The Fast Break

The most fundamental part of Red Auerbach's impressive and revolutionary offensive system was his emphasis on the fast break. The fast break is a fundamental basketball situation and strategy that requires the team to quickly move from the defensive side of the court to the offensive end before the opponents get to set up on defense. This usually results in the team outnumbering the defenders or creating defensive mismatches and confusion on the offense. And when that happens, it creates easy and quick baskets for the team because the defense has not set up properly or there are not enough defenders to prevent the offense from scoring.

The fast break is also how the team quickens the pace. Whenever a team decides that they want to run to trigger quick transition opportunities, they can put more points up on the board while wasting as little time as possible. Because the fast break happens when teams decide to increase the tempo and pace, it usually results in high-scoring outputs.

As simple as the fast break may sound, it was the foundation of what made Red Auerbach's Boston Celtics so fluid, deadly, and balanced as an offensive team. From 1959 to 1969, the Boston Celtics averaged 117 points a night because they never stopped running and attacking from the opening tip up to the final buzzer of the game. At one point, they even averaged 124.5 points per game because of the fluidity of their offensive attack.

Red Auerbach made use of all of his players' talents to trigger the fast break during the Boston Celtics' championship years. It all started with Bill Russell, who was his best player. Russell's defensive intensity and ability to grab rebounds made it easier for the Celtics to run a fast game. Because he could force bad shots while grabbing the misses without any help, Russell allowed all of his other teammates to run the floor hard the moment the ball left the hands of the shooter. And when Russell grabbed, the fast break came into play.

Bill Russell would usually hand the ball over to the point guard, who was either Bob Cousy or KC Jones, after he rebounded the ball. The Boston Celtics' point guards would always try to spot one of their open teammates running hard over at the other end for quick transition opportunities or even take the ball over to the other end of the floor to score baskets on their own whenever recovering defenders tried to cover the ones that were already waiting for passes up the floor. Showing that he could also make the passes, Russell would also throw outlets over to streaking players for easy open plays that only needed a few seconds to materialize.

The fast break was a strategy that worked well for Red Auerbach and was fit for his players. He always made sure that everyone on his team was well-conditioned to run the entire 48-minute stretch of the game. His guards were all capable of running the floor while his forwards were just as mobile as guards. He also kept his bench ready and conditioned to take over for the starters whenever they were needed to because running the entire game took a lot out of the players, even the ones with the best stamina.

The philosophy for Red Auerbach's team was simple: pass first and look for the shot as a last resort. Back then, point guards such as Bob Cousy and KC Jones were not as athletic as the likes of today's Russell Westbrook, John Wall, and Chris Paul to be able to take the ball from the backcourt all the way to the basket in a hurry. The first thing they had to do was to look up the floor to see if they had an open teammate that ran up ahead before them and reward them by passing the ball over to their side. It was only when the opposing defense had covered all of their options that Cousy, Jones, and the other guards were obliged to use their talent and creativity to look for shots. And for Cousy's case, he was one of the most ambidextrous and skilled finishers in the league despite his lack of size and athleticism.[xx]

While Red Auerbach had the personnel that was ready to run the fast break at any moment of the game, it was more important to have the running mindset. Cousy once said that Auerbach was happier if the team never had to call a single play the entire 48-minute stretch of the game because that meant that everyone on the team was dedicated to run the floor hard every time.

And if the players made a mistake, they never needed to look for Auerbach on the bench to ask whether he had a play ready for them. The simple task they had to do was to make sure they get possession of the ball back and run the break again. Cousy said that Auerbach liked it better when his players knew what they had to do on the floor without having to look at him for plays. That was what it meant to have a running mindset and philosophy.

As easy as it sounds, playing a fast break game was tougher than anyone realized. Some players would even conclude that it is tougher than playing a controlled half-court style. It takes another level of consciousness to play fast every second of the game or else it would lead to turnovers or botched plays. It was a mindset that not everyone was willing to get into because of how difficult it was. Having the proper personnel was one thing, but having the mindset to run the play at every open opportunity was another thing. It was something that Red

Auerbach had to drill into the minds of his players during practices and training camp.

Auerbach had a few key teachings when he was drilling the fast break into the minds of his players. He told them to never bounce the ball without a purpose.[xvii] This meant that a player should never put the ball down on the floor when he did not need to because the first thing he had to do was to look for an open teammate to pass the ball to.

In line with that thought, Red Auerbach always believed that a fast break style of play was no use if the players did not pass. He taught his players that passing the ball was the fastest way to advance it. In line with how players do not need to dribble the ball without a purpose, his guys should always look for the pass first if they wanted to play fast because the pass is always faster than even the fastest runner on the planet. And when the pass is not caught properly, it is almost always the fault of the passer and not the receiver. Because of this, Auerbach always made it a point to have his players train the way they passed the ball.

Because of how well the Celtics played their offense, they were nearly unstoppable. Red Auerbach only had seven basic plays for his team, but they were almost never used because of how well they were running the break. Everybody in the league knew what those seven plays were, but they were still unable to stop the Celtics because of their potent offensive attack.

Bruce Lee, a martial artist that was famous back in the 60's and early 70's, once said, "I fear not the man who has practiced 10,000 kicks once, but I fear the man who has practiced one kick 10,000 times." This meant that a man that has mastered one move was better than a man who knows thousands of moves but has never mastered one. And for the Red Auerbach's Boston Celtics, it did not matter whether they had hundreds of plays or only seven of them because they mastered those plays and their running style to such perfection that it was almost impossible to beat them. For Red, mastering how to run the break was better than knowing how to do hundreds of plays without perfecting them.

The best thing about the running style of play of the Boston Celtics was not only that they were winning championships but also that they were winning the hearts of crowds, not only in New England but also in the other parts of the world. The fast break made basketball a lot more fun to watch rather than the slow-paced half court style of play the rest of the league played.

This fast break style of play led to drastic changes in how the game was played on both ends of the floor. Red Auerbach once said that basketball is like a war because weapons are first developed before the defensive measures are thought up. When the Boston Celtics overwhelmed the basketball world with their fast offense, opposing teams were left confused on what to do on the defensive end. However, it ultimately led to an improvement in how teams tried to defend the fast break.

It took a while for defensive strategies against the transition attack to be developed. Coaches improved transition defenses by having their players get back on the defensive end without having to go in for an offensive rebound. The moment the ball left the hands of their shooter, other offensive players would run back on defense without even thinking they had a chance to get the ball back.

Some coaches would take a different approach and try to hound the initial ball-handler the moment he got the ball off the rebound.[xx] The pressure prevents the player, usually the point guard, from quickly running over to the other end. This also prevents him from getting a clear line of sight to make a pass to an open teammate that ran ahead of him up on the court. The changing style of defense was an indirect contribution that Red Auerbach's fast-breaking style brought to the basketball world.

As teams learned how to prevent the fast break over the years, the use of the style diminished as coaches reverted to a half-court style and a more controlled tempo. The use of the fast break style suddenly became a rarity during the 80's when teams were more inclined to use the pick-and-roll and isolation more frequently on the half court. However, the 80's version of the Los Angeles Lakers, ran by Magic Johnson, brought back the style and improved on the principles that Red Auerbach taught back in the 60's.

They proved that the fast break was still a deadly weapon to use in the NBA even though defenses had evolved to learn how to stop the strategy that once took the NBA by storm.

The 80's Lakers used the same formula of Red Auerbach's Celtics. They had a big-time rebounder in the likes of Kareem Abdul-Jabbar, who was their version of Bill Russell. Then Magic Johnson was their Bob Cousy and would even sometimes be the one to rebound the ball because he was 6'9". The moment he got the ball off the rebound or a pass from one of their other rebounders, he had guys like Byron Scott, James Worthy, and Michael Cooper filling the lanes as easy targets for his passes. It was more or less the same principles that Auerbach laid down in the 60's when he was coaching the Celtics to nine championship runs.

When it comes right down to it, any team that plays fast in today's NBA can trace its philosophies down to Red Auerbach's teachings about the fast break. The concept of securing the defensive rebound and having your wings run the floor while waiting for the pass from the point guard or outlet from the rebounder remain alive even though the three-point shot has become prevalent. The only difference in how today's fast break is being run is how it is finished because teams nowadays prefer their wings to run to the three-point line instead of the paint. However, everything else has stayed the same. Red Auerbach's Celtics were the innovators of arguably the most exciting brand of basketball in the history of the sport.

Defense: Effort and Hard Work

Back in the days when the Boston Celtics dominated in the 60's, defense was not as evolved as it is today. It was not until the 1979-80 season that the three-point line was instituted in the NBA. During the 60's, every shot you made, no matter how far it was, was only as good as a two-point basket. Because of that, it was easier to defend back then than it is in today's NBA because all that teams had to do was make sure opponents shot as far away from the basket as possible.

While it may have been easier to defend back then, it did not exactly mean that defending was simple. Players had to be more creative when they had to dribble their way to the basket or when they finished shots near the rim. That was when shots such as the finger roll and bank shot were revolutionized because defenders tried to get opposing players to shoot tougher shots as much as possible.

Red Auerbach's defensive tactics were not much different back then. The focus of the Boston Celtics' defense was making opponents shoot tougher baskets, which were usually the more inefficient perimeter jump shots. Life was made easier for Red and his team because they had Bill Russell, who was arguably the most dominant defensive player in the league.

No player in the league had the defensive abilities of Bill Russell. He was about 6'10" and was taller than almost any other starting center in the NBA save for rare seven-footers such as Wilt Chamberlain. Despite his size, he was more athletic and mobile than fellow centers. He could move and run the floor better than any other big man. Because of those tools, he was the league's premier defensive presence. He could cover ground with ease because of his mobility. He used his size and quickness to recover near the basket to make it difficult as much as possible for opponents to score. And because of his great timing and instincts, Russell was a great shot-blocker, though Red Auerbach would have preferred him to stay on the ground to contest baskets. Nevertheless, Red became a believer in Russell's revolutionary shot-blocking, which was not an official stat back then.

Arguably the only other center in the league that could contend with Bill Russell's defensive abilities was the 7'1" athletic freak of nature known as Wilt Chamberlain. While Wilt's athleticism and stamina are what legends are made of, he still had to focus his energy on plenty of other aspects of the game. He had to score, rebound, defend, and make plays. Meanwhile, Russell's focus was primarily geared towards making life tougher for opposing players to score and securing the misses after forcing bad shots. The occasional outlet pass was also an option for him, but Bill Russell was the premier defensive presence in the history of the NBA because he focused on that primary objective of his.

With Bill Russell manning the paint for Red Auerbach's Boston Celtics during the late 50's and 60's, he made the team arguably the most imposing defensive squad in the entire NBA. There were almost no easy shots for the opponents whenever Russell was on the floor to contest near the basket. With Bill Russell roaming the paint, the Celtics were able to force their opponents into taking less efficient perimeter jumpers rather than getting blocked or contested by the legendary defensive center near the basket. This was why, for many years during the 60's, the Celtics led the league in defensive rating.

In many ways, Red Auerbach's use of Bill Russell's defensive skills triggered the Boston Celtics' mastery as a defensive team. Before he was drafted, some of Russell's peers tried to tell him to play somewhere else and for a team that was defense-oriented instead of for the Celtics, whose primary focus was running the floor as much as possible. But Russell said that he would not change his stripes and would continue to play defense for Boston. And Red Auerbach himself told the center that he would be fit with the Boston Celtics' style of play.[xxi] This gave birth to an even more effective running game because of how

Russell could trigger fast-break opportunities with his defense and outlet passes.

While Bill Russell was their anchor on defense and was one of the initiators of their deadly fast break plays, the Celtics' defense was more than just their dominant center or the sum of their parts. Red Auerbach has laid the foundations of how to play proper defense on all of his players. And even when he did, he always emphasized the importance of making it more difficult for opponents to score by using effort and hard work on the defensive end.

Red Auerbach always preached to his players to never rest on defense.[xvii] Because the fast break offense required his players to be more conditioned than any other guys in the league, Auerbach also emphasized the importance of putting more effort on the defensive end than they did on their transition attack. Because of that, resting on defense was never an option.

What was also great about the Celtics was that Red Auerbach could afford to make all of his players put a lot of effort and hard work on the defensive end because of how deep his roster was. During the 1962-63 season, his Celtics were 11 men deep. Eight of those players played at least 20 minutes a night while only Bill Russell and Sam Jones played more than 30 minutes per game. Because of this, Auerbach's players were well-rested. He could afford to make them play hard on both ends of the floor because they had a lot of time to rest since the bench was as competitive as the starting unit.

The Boston Celtics were not merely relying on Bill Russell's defensive ability near the basket. The goal was to force tough perimeter shots, which the rest of the guys also tried to contest as much as they could. Auerbach often preached to his perimeter defenders to watch the ball-handler's hips instead of the ball. The ball may go one way and then a different way, but a player will always go to where his hips take him.

According to Red, a player cannot go anywhere without his hips, and that was precisely what defenders should watch for.[xvii] The perimeter defense made it hard for opponents to get to the basket because of how they impeded movement.

And if they were forced to take shots from the perimeter, defenders were always there to contest those shots.

Because of how Red Auerbach made it a focus for his teams to let the opposing squad take far and inefficient shots instead of easier looks near the basket, he was vehemently against the three-point shot when it was introduced to the NBA in 1979. He once called it a simple gimmick that was implemented only to attract television audience at a time when the league had bad ratings.[xxii]

Despite the initial adverse reaction to the three-point line, the NBA eventually learned to accept it openly. This included Red Auerbach, whose Boston Celtics during the 80's became one of the first teams in league history to use it proficiently and better than any other squad during that era. The growth of the three-point shot's usage has made Auerbach's defensive mantra of forcing players to shoot far away from the basket less effective than it was back then because advance analytics today show that the most efficient shots in the game are ones near the basket, which is obvious, and the three-point shot.

This new emphasis on the three-point shot has diminished the use of defensive big men. Teams would try to space the floor as much as possible to get the center out of the paint to open driving lanes or to make it easier for shooters to operate out on the perimeter. Had Bill Russell played in today's era, his defensive mastery might not have been as useful as it was back then because some players would prefer to shoot far away from the basket instead of near the rim. And floor-spacing centers would have tried to get Russell out of the paint.

Nevertheless, the implementation of the three-point shot did not make Bill Russell and Red Auerbach's defensive tactics useless. It might have been more effective back then to force opponents to shoot far away from the basket, but it would still work today because the most efficient shot in basketball is still the dunk or the layup at the rim despite the fact that the three-point shot has become increasingly popular. Blocking out the lane and contesting shots at the basket would still be the most fundamental aspect of defensive basketball in any other era of the NBA no matter how much the league has been trending towards the three-pointer.

While the way the 60's Boston Celtics defended may not work as effectively in today's NBA because of the emphasis on the three-pointer's usage, every other defensive basic that Auerbach preached back then still applies. This includes watching the ball-handler's hips instead of the ball and all sorts of other simple tactics that Red tried to drill into the brains of his players.

One such tactic that Red Auerbach taught to his players was an intangible aspect of the game. Whenever the referee decided that the opposing team should get possession of the ball because it went out of bounds, Auerbach would tell his players to give the ball slowly to the official instead of quickly to the other team because the extra time bought allowed the Celtics' defense to get into position.[xvii]

It was the little things like defensive fundamentals, hard work, and effort that what made the difference in Red Auerbach's defense. The fact that the Boston Celtics did not allow easy shots near the basket or from the perimeter made the team one of the best defensive squads in the 60's, and not just because Bill Russell was there to man the paint. Defense is, and was always, more about discipline, effort, and hard work. Any defensive strategy would be useless if the players did not put their backs into trying to stop the opposing team from scoring. And for Red, the fact that a player was motivated to play defense was already enough for him.

Chapter 6: Key Takeaways

Motivation

The fact that Red Auerbach was one of the best motivators in league history was what made him an exceptional leader to the point that even Bill Russell would say that it was his best trait. Anyone can be a genius basketball strategist. Plenty of other managers can pull off the moves that Red has done. However, not a lot of coaches can claim that they have become the great motivator that Auerbach was.

It is a universal truth in any organization or business that motivated employees and personnel would always yield the best results. A person unhappy, unfulfilled, and unmotivated to work hard is the worst type of employee because there is little to no incentive for him to try to improve his results and productivity.

But motivation is always a two-way street. While it may be important for employers to have employees that have the desire to be motivated and for the employees to try their best to improve their work, it also falls upon the leader to find ways to drive his personnel and to be there for them whenever they need him.

Red Auerbach was well aware of the fact that motivation was a give-and-take relationship. Known as a colorblind coach, he never cared about a player's race or color so long as he was skilled and motivated. Auerbach always tried to acquire players that were motivated themselves. However, it was also his job as the leader and coach of the team to keep his players motivated at all times.

The Boston Celtics of the 60's were always one of the most motivated teams because Red Auerbach tried different ways to motivate the different personalities on the team. Knowing that it takes different approaches to motivate people of different backgrounds and histories, Red never got tired of getting to know his players to know what made them tick and what got them to work harder.

Every season, Red Auerbach also used different ways to get his team to work harder because it was more difficult to motivate a man that was already at the apex of the mountain. To convince a person that was already on top to go even higher and to reach the clouds was the most difficult task for Auerbach to do every year. However, he was always able to pull it off and used pride as his primary weapon. By convincing his guys that being proud to be a champion every summer was the best feeling an athlete could get, Red Auerbach produced results every season and was able to get his players to win eight consecutive championships and a total of nine titles in ten years.

Motivation is the greatest tool a leader can have to produce the best results out of his employees and personnel. As great of a manager as he always was, Red Auerbach used motivation as a way to keep his players going and to make them improve their performance every season. A successful leader would always want the best out of his players knowing that it will yield the best results more often than not. And since motivation is a two-way street, both parties must do their part. And for Red Auerbach, he never failed to do his part to find what would keep his players going. Nine championship trophies would say that his players fulfilled their role as well.

Genius

Red Auerbach has always been a genius on an off the court. His mind helped revolutionize basketball. Primarily using the fast break as his weapon of choice, Auerbach changed the way the offense was being played because of how effective his running and transition game was. And because Red knew that defenses would later adjust to new offensive weapons, the way defense was being played also changed just to try to stop the Boston Celtics' fast break attack. On the court, his genius contributed a lot to how the game was being played on both ends of the floor. However, he also contributed more to the Celtics off the court.

Being the genius that he was, Red Auerbach orchestrated some of the biggest steals the league has ever seen on his way to forming championship teams for the Boston Celtics in different eras of the NBA. In 1956, he convinced the Rochester Royals to stay away from drafting Bill Russell by offering them a lucrative show for free. Russell became the single most dominant defensive force of his time, and the Royals could have been the ones that benefitted from his skills had they decided that having the Ice Capades for one week was not worth missing out on one of the best players in league history.

In 1970, Red Auerbach kept other teams from drafting Dave Cowens by acting like he was not interested in the future superstar center. During halftime of one of Cowens' college games, Auerbach left seemingly disgusted and disappointed just to make it seem like scouting the big man was not worth his time. The gamble worked, and nobody in the league drafted Dave Cowens before he was taken by the Celtics.

In 1978, Red Auerbach took advantage of a loophole in the rules to draft Larry Bird a year before he graduated from college. Two years later, he would complete the 1980's Big Three of the Celtics by orchestrating "The Steal of the Century." Red would trade the top overall pick to the Golden State Warriors to acquire star center Robert Parish and their third overall pick. He would then use that third pick to draft Kevin McHale, who he thought was the best player of the class of 1980. That move brought two future Hall of Famers to Boston for the price of a player that was not even half as accomplished as McHale or Parish.

It was those genius moves that made Red Auerbach a notorious name in the world of basketball. Those trades and off-the-court decisions brought the Boston Celtics a total of 16 NBA championships. Nine were from his coaching days, and the other seven were from the days when he was a general manager. Only one championship was without the intervention of Auerbach, though Danny Ainge, who was responsible for putting together that 2008 championship team, was one of his former players. In essence, Red Auerbach had an indirect hand in helping the Boston Celtics win their 17th championship trophy. And because of that, all of Boston's 17 NBA titles could trace their roots to Red Auerbach, the quintessential championship leader in the world of basketball.

The Fast Break

One of Red Auerbach's most significant contributions to the world of basketball was how he revolutionized the fast break. At a time when teams preferred to play a more controlled half-court game, Auerbach had his teams playing fast throughout the 48-minute stretch. Using quick transition baskets to his teams' advantage, Red could get the Celtics easy points when opposing defenses failed to get back on their defensive end of the floor.

Using Bill Russell as the anchor of a defensive strategy prevented teams from getting good looks at the basket. The center would initiate the fast break by rebounding misses and quickly giving the ball to his point guards. The point guard, who was either Bob Cousy or KC Jones, would look ahead to make a pass at a player that had already run up the floor or to find an open shot if the pass was not available. In some other cases, Bill Russell would even orchestrate the break himself by throwing quick outlet passes from his end over to the other end for easy transition baskets. That was essentially how Red Auerbach's fast break worked.

Though it may sound easy, not everyone in the league wanted to play as fast as the Boston Celtics. What made the fast break challenging to do over a 48-minute stretch like the Celtics did was the mental discipline and higher level of consciousness it took to be able to do it perfectly. Not everyone was as selfish as Red's Celtics were to be able to first look for the best pass instead of trying to take a shot. Not everyone could try to run the floor at every opportunity even though there was no assurance that he would get to score the ball himself on the break. And not everyone had the consciousness to quickly make a pass up the court to an open man without having to think about it. It never took more than a second for Auerbach's players to make the best possible decision on the fast break. And the way he was able to drill such a mindset into his players' brains was an experience that not everyone in the league was willing to take.

Because of the success that Red Auerbach's fast break had, several teams would follow suit. The 80's Los Angeles Lakers ran the fast break better than anyone did during that era. It yielded them five championships back then. The Mike D'Antoni Phoenix Suns were also one of the best running teams during the 2000's. While they were unable to win titles, they revolutionized the fast break into their own run-and-gun style of play.

Fast forward to the second decade of the new millennium, and teams suddenly went back to a quick pace style of play. Because the Steve Kerr version of the Golden State Warriors loved to run, the fast break evolved into an art where the players would rather sprint towards the three-point line instead of filling out the lanes in transition. Because defenses were more inclined to protect the paint during transition, the three-pointer was wide open for them to take and make.

While today's fast break may seem a little different from how Red Auerbach's Boston Celtics played, the elements remain the same. All of the league's running teams in history can trace their roots down to the basics of the 60's version of the championship green team. While the addition of the three-point line changed the way it was being played, it is still essentially the same. The end goal was to run towards the other half of the court to get quick baskets before the defense could get back or to even set up. Red Auerbach introduced and revolutionized it while other coaches only perfected it to fit the changing times.

Conclusion

Known not only as the greatest coach in NBA history but also as the best winner in professional basketball, Red Auerbach's influence transcended his contributions to the Boston Celtics all the way to how the game is being played today. If you look at it, many elements of today's NBA basketball was influenced directly or indirectly by what Red Auerbach did back in the day.

The way offense is being played is an example of how Red Auerbach indirectly influenced basketball. The Boston Celtics' fast break offense made defenses work harder to prevent transition opportunities. This led to teams going back to using isolation and pick-and-roll plays on the half court set more often than they did the fast break. And when the half court failed to work because of how slowly teams liked to grind the pace out, teams would return to playing fast with the addition of the three-point line. The way the game is being played on the offensive end in today's NBA can be traced to the effects of how Auerbach revolutionized the way offense was being played and how the defense reacted to the introduction of his fast break offense.

Introducing the concepts of the sixth man and role player was also one of the ways Red changed basketball. At a time when other coaches would want to have their star players hog all the minutes and possessions, Auerbach paved the way for team basketball and balanced lineups by empowering his bench and players that were not stars.

Auerbach would always have one of his stars play off the bench to lead the second unit while the starters were resting and used their fresh legs to overwhelm the opposing team. And knowing that not everyone can produce the same numbers that stars could, he allowed his other players to flourish by assigning them roles. Everyone on the team had a defined role to play, and it did not matter whether the player was a star or the last person on the bench. The Boston Celtics were a balanced group because everyone was a role player in their own right.

Coaches would later follow Red Auerbach's example by having certain players play roles they specialized at. There were designated defenders, rebounders, shooters, and sparks off the bench. Other teams would even try to emulate the Celtics by having one of their best players lead the second unit to make sure they would not lose any production when the starters were resting. And while some stars have the capacity and skill to do everything out on the floor, coaches would now emphasize the importance of playing team basketball and letting other players contribute in any way they could. This was a winning formula that coaches started to emulate because Red Auerbach was able to bring nine championships to Boston.

One can also say that basketball may not have been what it is today had Red Auerbach not chosen to cross barriers. Known as a colorblind leader at a time when there were barriers between races, Red never cared about the color of his players' skin so long as they were motivated contributors. He would draft Chuck Cooper, who is known as the NBA's first black player. In 1964, he fielded the NBA's first all-black starting five. Two years after that, he stepped down from coaching and gave the reins to Bill Russell, who became the first African-American coach not only in the NBA but all four of American's primary professional sporting leagues.

But when asked if he did all that for publicity or to leave a legacy in the NBA, Red Auerbach always claimed that he never did it on purpose. It was only because he thought that it was the best move basketball-wise to cross racial barriers. He always thought that Cooper was a good basketball player even back in college. When he fielded the first all-black starting five, it was because it was his most balanced five players. And when he gave the coaching hat to Bill Russell in 1966, it was because he trusted him to lead the team both as the coach and the best player on the team.

By making those moves based on basketball decisions and not for any publicity stunt, Red Auerbach paved the way for people of different colors and races to make it to the NBA based on their abilities as basketball players or coaches. Today, the NBA has become predominantly black and has attracted star talent from all over the globe. Even many coaches are African-American. And when it comes down to it, the first person to give African-Americans a shot at becoming great in the NBA was Red Auerbach.

But beyond all the championships won, the concepts and strategies revolutionized, and the legacies left behind was a cigar-smoking man that had so much passion for the game to the point that he was willing to get into the faces of referees and opposing players, coaches, and owners. Red Auerbach made the NBA the spectacle it is right now not only because he made it fun to watch through the Celtics' fantastic way of playing, but also because of how he made it a show with his colorful personal touch.

The way he cared about his players and team also allowed the Boston Celtics franchise to grow as one of the first true and stable organization in the league. Red Auerbach became the true embodiment of the Boston Celtics just as how the Boston Celtics became the embodiment of what Red was. He was a revolutionary, an innovator, a champion, and an influential figure. More importantly, he always looked ahead to the future and made sure he not only left the Celtics lasting legacies but also something to work on to make sure they would stay stable as a franchise.

Beyond those nine championships and several Hall of Fame products was a man that truly embodied what it meant to be arguably the most influential figure in the history of the NBA. The name "Red Auerbach" has been synonymous with greatness. And when you look what he has accomplished and what he has contributed to the league, those nine or even 16 championships barely scratch the surface of what Red meant to the NBA. Basketball would truly not be what it is right now if it were not for Arnold Jacob Auerbach.

Final Word/About the Author

I was born and raised in Norwalk, Connecticut. Growing up, I could often be found spending many nights watching basketball, soccer, and football matches with my father in the family living room. I love sports and everything that sports can embody. I believe that sports are one of most genuine forms of competition, heart, and determination. I write my works to learn more about influential athletes and coaches in the hopes that from my writing, you the reader can walk away inspired to put in an equal if not greater amount of hard work and perseverance to pursue your goals. If you enjoyed *Red Auerbach: The Inspiring Life and Leadership Lessons of One of Basketball's Greatest Coaches,* please leave a review! Also, you can read more of my works on *Roger Federer, Novak Djokovic, Andrew Luck, Rob Gronkowski, Brett Favre, Calvin Johnson, Drew Brees, J.J. Watt, Colin Kaepernick, Aaron Rodgers, Peyton Manning, Tom Brady, Russell Wilson, Michael Jordan, LeBron James, Kyrie Irving, Klay Thompson, Stephen Curry, Kevin Durant, Russell Westbrook, Anthony Davis, Chris Paul, Blake Griffin, Kobe Bryant, Joakim Noah,*

Scottie Pippen, Carmelo Anthony, Kevin Love, Grant Hill, Tracy McGrady, Vince Carter, Patrick Ewing, Karl Malone, Tony Parker, Allen Iverson, Hakeem Olajuwon, Reggie Miller, Michael Carter-Williams, John Wall, James Harden, Tim Duncan, Steve Nash, Draymond Green, Kawhi Leonard, Dwyane Wade, Ray Allen, Pau Gasol, Dirk Nowitzki, Jimmy Butler, Paul Pierce, Manu Ginobili, Pete Maravich, Larry Bird, Kyle Lowry, Jason Kidd, David Robinson, LaMarcus Aldridge, Derrick Rose, Paul George, Kevin Garnett, Chris Paul, Marc Gasol, Yao Ming, Al Horford, Amar'e Stoudemire, DeMar DeRozan, Isaiah Thomas, Kemba Walker and Chris Bosh in the Kindle Store. If you love basketball, check out my website at claytongeoffreys.com to join my exclusive list where I let you know about my latest books and give you lots of goodies.

Like what you read? Please leave a review!

I write because I love sharing the stories of influential coaches like Red Auerbach with fantastic readers like you. My readers inspire me to write more so please do not hesitate to let me know what you thought by leaving a review! If you love basketball, or productivity, check out my website at claytongeoffreys.com to join my exclusive list where I let you know about my latest books. Aside from being the first to hear about my latest releases, you can also download a free copy of *33 Life Lessons: Success Principles, Career Advice & Habits of Successful People*. See you there!

Clayton

References

[i] "Red Auerbach". *Jockbio.com*. Web.
[ii] Ryan, Bob. "Red was just full of color". *Boston.com*. 30 October 2006. Web.
[iii] "Red Auerbach". *Notable Biographies*. Web.
[iv] "Farewell to a basketball legend Red Auerbach: 1917-2006". *NBA.com*. 28 October 2006. Web.
[v] Schwartz, Larry. "Celtics tried to pass on ultimate passer". *ESPN*. Web.
[vi] Hilton, Lisette. "Auerbach's Celtics played as a team". *ESPN*.
[vii] Wolff, Alexander. "The road not taken". *Sports Illustrated*. 27 December 2004. Web.
[viii] Parquet, Professor. "The story of how rookie phenom Larry Bird led the NBA's greatest turnaround season". *Celtics Blog*. 7 January 2015. Web.
[ix] Surette, Chaz. "Boston Celtics: 10 greatest moves during Red Auerbach's tenure". *Bleacher Report*. 20 September 2011. Web.
[x] Shouler, Ken. "The consummate coach". *ESPN*. Web.
[xi] "Red Auerbach's leadership secret to winning 9 titles in 11 years". *Light House*. Web.
[xii] Russell, Bill. *Second Wind*. Ballantine Books, 1979. Print.
[xiii] "The Celtics' New Motivator". *New York Times*. 16 November 1978. Web.
[xiv] "When Bill Russell writes about Red Auerbach". *ESPN*. 21 October 2009. Web.
[xv] Atkin, Ross. "Boston Celtics' Red Auerbach, man with a championship touch". *The Christian Science Monitor*. 8 June 1984. Web.
[xvi] Adande, JA. "The truth isn't always black or white for Celtics". *ESPN*. 19 December 2007. Web.
[xvii] Rogin, Gilbert. "They all boo when Celtics legend Red Auerbach sits down". *Sports Illustrated*. 18 September 2015. Web.
[xviii] Webber, Alan. "Red Auerbach on management". *Harvard Business Review*. March 1987. Web.
[xix] "Red Auerbach and helping players reach their potential". *ASLAN Training*. 24 October 2015. Web.
[xx] McCallum, Jack. "The breaks of the game". *Sports Illustrated*. 11 November 1991. Web.
[xxi] Cacciola, Scott. "Red Auerbach told Bill Russell: 'I'm the coach and you'll fit'". *New York Times*. 24 June 2017. Web.
[xxii] Eger, Isaac. "The NBA's love affair with the three-pointer: thrilling fans, frustrating big men". *Timeline*. 18 May 2016. Web.

Made in the USA
San Bernardino, CA
23 August 2018